Praise for

Yet Will I Trust Him

We all love to celebrate victories, but not every story has such a fairy tale ending. So what happens when the prayer goes seemingly unanswered, the miracle never comes, or the mountain never moves? *Yet Will I Trust Him* walks you through such a journey. Through Kelly's personal story, you will be inspired and encouraged to never stop trusting in God no matter the outcome. Get ready to be challenged and your faith to be built as you read through the pages of this powerful book!

- Dustin Delino, author of *Shoulders to Stand On*

I hope you enjoy getting to know Kelly and hearing about his journey. He shares his heartfelt emotions through loss and disappointment time after time, yet still trusting God and standing on his promises. He will expose the roller coaster ride of emotions, excitement and painful heartache over and over. *Yet Will I Trust Him* will take you through a man's perspective on loss resulting from several miscarriages. Kelly's raw and real expressions of losing one of the desires of his heart will draw you in and encourage you and strengthen your faith as you walk through your own trials and disappointments.

- Shannon Segura, wife

Yet Will I Trust Him is an emotionally raw and honest account of life's unfortunate blows and God's faithfulness through the tumultuous and heart breaking. Kelly skillfully pens his journey through a series of loss and faith-building prayer and grief. His tenacity and girt to hold on to God's truth is sure to leave you inspired and bring you to your knees.

- Nathan Sam, worship leader

YET WILL I TRUST HIM

A STORY OF PERSEVERANCE AND FAITH

KELLY R. SEGURA

WESTBOW PRESS®
A DIVISION OF THOMAS NELSON & ZONDERVAN

WestBow Press books may be ordered through booksellers or by contacting:

WestBow Press
A Division of Thomas Nelson & Zondervan
1663 Liberty Drive
Bloomington, IN 47403
www.westbowpress.com
1 (866) 928-1240

ISBN: 978-1-5127-8212-7 (sc)
ISBN: 978-1-5127-8213-4 (hc)
ISBN: 978-1-5127-8211-0 (e)

Library of Congress Control Number: 2017905140

Print information available on the last page.

WestBow Press rev. date: 05/24/2017

CONTENTS

ACKNOWLEDGEMENTS

I would like to dedicate this book to my wonderful family who has been with me through every step of this journey. Specifically, I would like to thank my wonderful wife Shannon; you have taught me how to trust and love. To my son Dylan, thank you for letting me father you. You have healed me in many areas. I would also like to thank my mom and dad; you are both the jewels refined by fire. Your perseverance is of biblical proportions. Thank you.

I would like to also thank my pastor, Todd Menard, for his inspirational in-the-trenches leadership. He has lifted me with his shepherd staff and put me in greener pastures. I must also thank my friend Steve Himel who constantly reminded me of an absolute in my searching for answers- God is for me. Additionally, I want to thank Francis Martin, Family Life Church's founding pastor, who wrote *Hung by the Tongue* and has been an inspiration to many all over the world. His advice and wisdom has been so important to me. I would also like to thank my friends and family who have helped me with the editing and finishing of this book: Dustin Delino who authored an inspirational book called *Shoulders to Stand On* and helped me in the editing of this book; Mary Leblanc, another friend Rachel Marquet and my father-in-law, A.J. Dore', who both helped with the editing process, Anna Gumpert for the great job she did on the graphic design and pictures for this book, and Alice Viator who helped with the final editing process. I would also like to thank all of my friends- those I have mentioned and those I have not- I love and appreciate you, too.

FOREWORD

The Bible says in 2 Corinthians 1:4, "He comforts us in all our troubles so that we can comfort others. When they are troubled, we will be able to give them the same comfort God has given us" (*NLT*). The content of this book is in essence a fulfillment of this very verse! I, unlike most of you who will be reading this book, have had the opportunity to have a front row seat and to witness much of this book as it unfolded. I've been a personal friend and pastor to the author, Pastor Kelly, for several years now. I know that the contents of this book are not a bunch of biblical intellectual head knowledge, but personal life experience that has flowed out of his heart and walk with the Lord. I've had the chance to see Kelly get knocked down again and again, but then by God's grace get up again and again. I've witnessed his great discouragement during dire situations, but then his rising out of the ash heap into victory. As Pastor Kelly unpacks the highs and lows of his personal life experiences and the revelations the Lord has given him throughout his journey, I know you'll be drawn into his story, as well as be able to identify with his personal everyday struggles and frustrations. I think this book is unique in that it is filled with biblical truth, but it is also filled with life lessons that you can apply in your personal life. I've watched the Lord use the adversity and tribulations Pastor Kelly has faced to forge him into the great man of God he is today! The adversity and trials he has faced have made him better not bitter! I believe God will use the content of this book to help you become a great man or woman of God as well. In your adversity, these truths will help you become better instead of bitter. If you will take the time to read this book, I know you will be greatly inspired and encouraged in your personal journey. My prayer is that as the Lord personally comforts and encourages your heart, you will do as 2 Corinthians 1:4 says and turn around and comfort others with the same comfort you received from the Lord by reading this book.

Todd Menard
Lead Pastor, Family Life Church

INTRODUCTION

Throughout this book, I will talk to you about spiritually leaning on and trusting God despite suffering and doubting that leads to joy and believing. I hope that in sharing my journey, you will see that while in the Christian faith there are many trials and tribulations, I've learned to persevere with the Scriptures which has given me life and power. There may come a time in your life when all you have is what you believe- and even at that point, you may question what you believe. My story is not the norm in Christianity- I have to admit that- and what I experienced may not sell books. This kind of story should not expect to lead to giant altar calls for salvation. In fact, I'm sure many who read this book maybe plagued with discouragement, but to others I'm sure it will give some type of clarity, and to others still it may bring encouragement. When I think about the book of Job, it doesn't seem very encouraging until we find ourselves in a crippling trial.

The great Apostle Peter tells us in 1 Peter 4:12, *"Beloved, think it not strange concerning this fiery trial which is to try you, as though some strange thing happened to you" (KJV).* While The Bible does not say how long this fiery trial will last, I can tell you the trial sometimes worsens. You know it's bad when a fiery trial almost seems like the expectation for your life. My brother-in-law once told me, "If God told you the whole picture of why the things are happening to you maybe you wouldn't accept His plan. Kelly, if you knew you would experience these miscarriages all for the sole purpose, hypothetically speaking, of maybe three people getting saved, you probably would say, 'No.'" Instantly, I felt the presence of the Holy Spirit. He went on to say, "If your dad got cancer so healthy people can realize how grateful they should be for having health to serve Him, you would probably say, 'No,' but we have to resolve to put God's plans before ours." The way God chooses to do something or allows something in our life has to be greater than the desire to have what we want. When you signed up for Christianity, you signed up for fiery furnaces, lions' dens, shipwrecks, and Red Sea experiences, but the good news is God delivered His people from them all. Remember this- trials bring God. The more trials, the more God. The greater the storm, the greater the plan and purpose.

I will have to say that what I am writing is therapy for me. In this book my plan is to pour out my heart, pain and all. I really feel that I owe it to you to explain my journey in an honest way. This journey is one of growth and learning; our pain and disappointments are where the growth happens. I want to tell you upfront that in our Christian walk there comes a time when we will be forced to come to terms with what we believe. Things will come, and they will be the litmus test that will show us who we are and what we believe about God, His purpose, and His plans. There are a lot of things that come our way that may not line up with what we at first believe, but if we are wise we will not give in to the unanswered questions, but rather dig deeper into the answer which is Jesus Christ. As of right now, I still don't have a reason for not being able to have a baby on this side of heaven. I have children; they are just with Jesus. I know you may be thinking, "Poor man. He has to think that to help him feel better." I can assure you that is not the case; I can prove it to you, and I will explain later.

What if I asked you if God can trust you with pain? You see, God is good all the time, but it's up to us to find how good in our greatest crisis. Perspective sounds like a religious cop out. It can make a good sermon outline and will get an occasional amen depending on how hard the preacher can sell it, but what about how you truly feel at home in bed the Monday night when the hype wears off? I want to walk together with you in this journey of my personal greatest disappointments and those of my family. This will apply somewhere, someday, in some way to what you face. I would have to say that I kicked and screamed through some of this process. Well, let me say it better- through most of it. But through it all, the Lord showed himself true because He never leaves us nor forsakes us, as the Bible says. My intention is not to preach to you or give you an answer; my goal is to be honest and to encourage you to go deeper in your relationship with Jesus Christ. My greatest desire, which is to be a daddy, is still not realized. Unless God does a miracle, it will never be here. So now what? Maybe you can say that you feel the same way, that you have been pleading with God for your greatest desire to be met, and it looks impossible. Listen, I used to get so frustrated sometimes when I read the Bible and God would make it sound so easy to just believe, but His will will always take front and center before our desire, and we have to accept that. Listen, I take my relationship with God literally, and you need to know that religion is a cheap counterfeit. In a relationship, it is two sided, and we have the privilege to enter into a glorious living relationship, where we can discuss our disappointments, frustrations, and joys with our heavenly Father through our elder brother Jesus. Friend, please don't take that for granted. I say this because eternity is the greatest gift you and I can receive. Don't lose sight of the fact that you and I don't have to spend eternity in Hell apart from God. Don't forfeit your soul on a desire that goes unmet. If God never answered another prayer, we are still saved from the wrath to come. In all of our disappointments, God still loves us, and He is big enough to take our gripes and fits that we throw. He understands, but I want to add this caveat - in our frustrations and fussing we are still talking to a King, so we must always be reverent. Frustrations will come and anger us, and we will be tempted to allow emotions to speak louder than they should. Not only are we talking to a King, but we are also talking to the lover of our souls. He is the one who gave it all. Don't let your prayer list be a tool that holds God against the wall. Believe me like some have said, "He is a Lion that cannot be tamed." God cannot be manipulated. While this may frustrate us, this is indeed a blessing because God cannot be talked into turning His back on us.

Sit back and allow me to bare my soul, and I hope this will help you. God has a purpose and a plan in all that we go through. I am still seeking it out through this writing. Maybe, just maybe, through my pain God will use it to help you see your own circumstances a little differently.

You may be wondering why the title *Yet Will I Trust Him*. The thing I have come to realize is that much like the book of Job, perspective is key. I am not saying God will slay me or kill me. What I am saying is that as a Christian I know that God's plans and purposes should override my plans and purposes every time. Sometimes that may feel like you are being sawed in two, but God is more concerned about His will, His plan, and His purpose than my comfort and that helps me because I prefer His plan rather than mine. My greatest desire is to have a baby, and that is a fact, but I have come to seek God's glory; I want His will to overpower mine. Everything in our lives- good or bad- has to sift through God's hands. My desire had to filter through His hands and knowing that is why I smile every day. I trust God more through these heartbreaks because I have an understanding that I didn't have before. My prayer is that when you finish reading this you, too, will have a new mindset in dealing with whatever comes your way. The Bible says in Isaiah 40:9, *"Get yourself up on a high mountain…[and declare] 'Here is Your God'" (NASB)*. I want to encourage you to climb up from the rubble of circumstance, get your footing, stand firm and look at every problem and verbally declare, "Here is My God."

Let me pray for you before we start.

Father, I come to you in the name that is above every name, my savior Jesus Christ. First of all, I acknowledge that without your help I cannot do this. Seriously, I need your help here, Lord. I have never written a book, but I ask that you would use this for your glory, and that my friend who is reading this will drop their guard towards you. I pray, Lord, that we will get a greater understanding and desire to make your will the most important aspect of our lives. Help us rise above our Isaacs. Lord, I acknowledge that I still can't wrap my brain around the why, but I pray through this work that we will learn to trust in you fully. God, you are good in all your ways. Just give us eyes to see, ears to hear, and hearts to receive by faith what you want us to learn in our greatest hurts. Lord, change us to not be circumstantial but unconditional in all that we are towards you. I thank you for your patience, kindness, long suffering, and your security. Amen.

ONE

I Am the Very Miracle I'm Believing For

And Jesus said to him, "'If You can?' All things are possible to him who believes."
(Mark 9:23 NASB)

I would like to begin by saying that I believe this verse with all my heart- no matter what I have experienced or will experience- however, I didn't get to this place overnight. We'll look more deeply into this verse shortly, but first let me begin my story.

My mom and dad were childhood sweethearts. They have liked one another since they were twelve-years-old and have been married since they were nineteen. If there is any couple who deserved to have a full quiver, it is my mom and dad; instead, they had seven total miscarriages over a period of ten years. There were two before me, and then five after me. The third miscarriage was twins. My mom lost one of the twins two weeks before she lost the other one. So with seven miscarriages and eight children lost, they took all the love they had and gave it to me. While this love seems like an obvious response, their rock-solid faith may not. You would think that their faith would have wavered and would have been a difficult topic to discuss with my mom and dad, as well as myself, but they have tremendous faith- and we would need it for the fight of our lives that we would encounter approximately thirty years later.

Even while my mom was pregnant with me, the doctors told my mom and dad that there was a very slim chance that I would be born, and if so, I would be severely deformed. They expected that these deformities would be so severe that I could possibly have a nose or an ear missing or even no neck. Contrary to medical opinion, I was born on July 29, 1977 without any deformities. I was born and am perfectly normal- even though that is debatable to those that know me. I would find out later in life that I had escaped the jaws of what the doctors would call a genetic problem that would typically stop birth in the womb. My brothers and sisters were not so fortunate. It was God's plan and purpose that I came into existence while he had another plan for my siblings.

Now, let's take a look at the verse in Mark. While I have not experienced this in every area of my life, I still believe it with all my heart. The verse says, *"'If You can?' All things are possible to him who believes" (Mark 9:23 NASB).* In this verse, Jesus is speaking to the father of a demon possessed boy who asks Jesus to free him if He can. Now Jesus repeats his statement as a question, "If you can?" and that is a question for you and me. "If you can?" is a question asking us something very telling. Jesus is asking us if some things seem so huge, so earth-shaking that we would have to ask, "Can I truly believe this?" What is it in your life that has drained you to a place that you would say, "I have spent all of my belief in this area, and I don't know if I can believe to receive what I am asking for?" Is it healing for a loved one? Maybe it is a situation that in the natural is impossible? My friend, that is when God is at His best. Can we hold on in spite of what we see, in spite of the lack of evidence that this will change? Do we have the audacity to still believe? Because if we do Jesus is thundering back saying, *"All things are possible to them that believe" (Matthew 19:26 KJV)*. I am not saying that our situation will change and that we have a blank check to name it and claim it because that is a trap of the enemy of our soul to beat us up and say we just don't have enough faith. Believe me, we can drive ourselves crazy, beat ourselves up, and shoulder something we shouldn't. A great friend of mine Steve Himel encouraged me through the trials I would later face. When I was looking for a miracle, he would remind me, "Kelly, you are the very miracle you are believing for. You are living proof that a genetic problem can't stop God." He was essentially being the voice of Jesus and asking me the same question, "Can you believe?"

I am grateful for the upbringing I received. Growing up as an only child from a child's perspective can seem lonely yet amazing because all efforts are focused on that one child. Kids love being the recipient of that kind of attention. There are many perks to being an only child. There is no need to share with siblings- neither toys, nor food, and most importantly love. I was drenched in love and for that I am so grateful. I now know that the long hugs from my parents were hugs of gratefulness to God for allowing me to come into this world. I also remember the long stares from my parents as they would watch me play; they were stares of gratitude to God that I was able to play and run normally. I now know that the only reason I was allowed to live is for the grace of God. My childhood is marked by being raised by parents who were grateful to God, and they showered that gratefulness on me. What a privilege! I see so many today who take children and having children for granted. I want to pause for a second just to give glory to God Almighty for answering the prayers of my mom and dad. I look back on all that they have done in my life and the sacrifices they have made and are still making, and I, too, am grateful that He heard their cry. Thirty years later I would have the same cry. It is with great awe and wonder that I thank God that He so graciously allowed them to experience the birth of a child. As a parent, you want the best for your children, but as a grown up child looking at my parents today, I am blessed to see that God gave them their desire. The Bible says that children are a gift from God. Let me ask you a question: "Are you grateful for your children whom God has given you? Do you see them as inconveniences in your life?" As I live without a biological child, I would love to have your challenges. When I hear the complaints of the late nights and all the other everyday things that can be tiresome, I tell God, "I'll take that, Lord." There is something that we must all understand in our life circumstances, and that is perspective. This is a key to our life and living that can help us in our journey of life. I will confess my sin to you, and that sin is struggling with perspective. I truly believe if we can learn this early, then it will help us in every other area of your life. My eternal perspective was a key that unlocked the door to coping with my tragedy. Our perspective is a gift from God.

During my childhood, my dad worked in the oil field and so worked very long hours. My mom tells me how she would get me to sleep before my dad would come in after dispatching all afternoon into the night. When he came home, he would wake me up to play, and she would get aggravated because she would have to try to put me back to sleep again. Then as I got older, I can remember my mom waking me up in the middle of the night, and I would find myself sitting across the table from my dad eating honey buns. While that might seem odd and you may think I needed my sleep- and I would agree with you- these are some of my most cherished memories.

My mom knew my dad very well and knew that though he loved me and wanted to spend time with me, but he would also work equally hard at his job as he would at being a dad because my grandfather had also been a hard worker and had instilled that in my dad. My dad is a faithful man in whatever he does. Throughout my childhood, he worked at the same company he had begun with soon after he graduated high school; for a time this company was only ten minutes away from our house, but later he was transferred about an hour away. This made our time together more precious. Despite how committed he was to his job, he worked around my baseball schedule where he wasn't just a fan, but also my baseball coach. He was also my sparring partner throughout my years of karate. One time I actually cracked his ribs, but he took it and said while hunched over and grasping for breath, "Good kick, Kel!" The reason my mom would wake me up to eat with him and the reason my dad adjusted his schedule to my activities was not because they had to, but because they wanted to. Although he worked a lot, I can't remember him missing any important event or activity; I can't remember one time that I needed him, and he wasn't there. I can't remember one baseball game when he wasn't coaching me from third base; I can't remember one karate tournament when he was not there telling me, "Kelly, keep your hands up." I could be wrong, but I certainly don't remember; if he did, God's grace covered it. After working what were sometimes 12 and 14 hour days, he had one thing on his mind when he got off of work and that was to spend time with his wife and little boy. Sometimes my dad would come home only to be greeted by a mob of teenagers- the perfect number of people for football teams- who still wanted him to be quarterback. The problem with that is we played tackle sometimes and Mississippi Rush which means sometimes he would get tackled or forced to scramble for his life, but he always did it.

My mom was also at every game. She was the score keeper, the team mom, the statistic recorder, and the photographer. My mom also substituted at my school so she could be close to me. As I grew up, I was somewhat of a "mama's boy" for which I don't apologize. When my mom dropped me off at school, we waved for what seemed like hours. I waved as she dropped me off and made the little turn around, came back up the road, and turned off at the end of the street. As I got a little older I still secretly tried to wave behind my back so the other kids wouldn't see because one of my teachers had let me in on a little secret. She told me that the other kids were teasing me behind my back. I was just so close to my parents that being away from them was painful for me; it is because I was captured by love. Later in life, I bought a house a couple of houses down from my parents. Even now, if we leave for work at the same time, I will see her and still wave as she passes in front of my house until she turns down the end of the street. I guess some things never change.

Back to my childhood- I can remember walking along a brick wall at school rubbing my finger along the mortar crying and wishing I was at home, not because I hated school but because I missed my mom. My mom knew it was difficult for me so sometimes she would come and park at the hospital across the street and watch me play. She did that so I would know she was there and feel a little better, and she also did it because she missed seeing me, too. Nowadays with all these new parenting philosophies, people may be shocked and think that is unhealthy. I must say I totally disagree. In today's world, I am seeing more selfishness in parenting. In many cases, the kids are forced to take the backseat to the parents, and it is producing a cold-hearted society. Kids grow up feeling unloved and unvalued. I see so many men and ladies now that I am older who are crushed in the spirit because of the rejection they felt as children. There is nothing wrong with loving your children and smothering them with love.

I honestly don't remember seeing the pain in my mom's and dad's eyes while they were going through all those miscarriages, but maybe that's why they squeezed me so tightly and always held me closely. Now that I have experienced such pain during my own battle with miscarriages, I only pray when I squeezed back during those hugs it helped with their pain. I always wanted a brother or a sister, and I used to think that one day I wanted to have many children of my own. I wasn't disappointed with being an only child, but I wanted to give the love I had received to my own children. I also wanted to give my parents many grandchildren to love; I wanted to alleviate some of the pain they had gone through and to reward them for doing such a great job with me. I know you want what's best for your children, but as an adult you end up wanting what's best for your parents. I also wanted that for my kids; they would have had the best grandparents. I remember as I grew into my teenage years my desire grew stronger, and I couldn't wait to get married and have a huge family. Children had become my greatest desire.

As I grew into a teenager, I was just as mischievous as any other teenager. I went to catechism, but to be honest, I really did not like it. I was a trouble maker in those classes, and for that, I truly am sorry to all the teachers I had. Looking back I appreciate the teachers who took the time to teach us. There was one time when I posed some questions to one of the priests. He was sitting in on our class, and we were able to ask anything we wanted so I asked something that is of interest to most teenagers. I asked about the beasts in the book of Revelation and the mark on the right hand or forehead; I also asked about the harlot that God will destroy with the cup in her hand. Questions like this have always appealed to me. The priest told me not to worry about things like that, and I told him disrespectfully that he just didn't know the answer. (Once again, I am sorry for that.) The priest told me I should do some penance for being disrespectful by washing his car. My parents were also called and informed of my disrespect, but instead of being angry with me, they believed that the priest should have answered my questions. My parents, I guess, were just happy I was engaging. Needless to say, I didn't finish catechism and never made my confirmation.

I had a cousin who was younger and who grew up in a Baptist church. He and my uncle played softball for a church league, and they often invited us to play. (Many years later I would have the privilege of officiating this cousin's wedding.) Eventually, my dad and I joined my uncle and my cousin in their church softball league, and we had a great time. As a teenager, I was always interested in the things of God; I just didn't know where to begin looking and where to find answers. Nearly every Sunday, my cousin invited us to their church, and while we typically said no, one Sunday we had a different answer; that Sunday changed the course of my family. On this Sunday, the pastor honored everyone who participated in the softball league. Afterwards he preached the gospel, and for the first time I felt like I was beginning to understand it. My mom and dad loved it, and we continued to attend. One Sunday after we began attending regularly, my mom, dad, and I responded to the end of service invitation; my response was purely emotional and religious, but my mom's and dad's were real. They always loved God in their own way, but that day they entered into a deeper relationship with the Lord because they had really come to understand the gospel.

One day we watched a movie on the rapture that was made in the 1970's. That was an eye opener for me, and it really cemented my desire to learn about the end times much like my questions to the priest years earlier. I would love to say at that moment I came to know the Lord, but that would be quite some years later. I am so grateful that the gospel reached my family. The gospel of Jesus Christ is the good news, and I am thankful, looking back, that it was always being placed before me. I went to youth group, and I learned a lot. I had a great youth pastor, Tommy Bell, and he truly understood where I was coming from. He knew I was a worldly little heathen and yet he loved me anyway. He deposited a lot of time in me aside from the youth group, and I am grateful for that. His influence in my life would help shape my patience for troubled people throughout my years in ministry. Although I appreciated having a youth group to go to, the pull of the world was too great, and I jumped in head-first and indulged in everything that came my way. I won't take the time to divulge my sinful details, but they were about as bad as you can imagine. I did everything there was to do starting at the age of fifteen years old. I indulged in drugs, alcohol, and sex; however, my mom and dad really didn't know the extent of my ways since I was very careful to keep it hidden. My upbringing was top notch, but so were my sinful ways. The sins I chose, I chose to drink down like water. Today when I see teenagers doing sinful things, many people say that it is their parents' fault for not raising them correctly. Sometimes this may be the case, but in my case, my ways were my ways and not reflective of my parents at all. I was a recipient of a tremendous childhood; I just wanted to do what I wanted to. My sinful nature was large and in charge. However, despite all of the sin I indulged in, I always had the conviction of the Lord upon me. I always felt bad coming home drunk or high, and I would always let my parents know I was home. We had a rule that I honored, and it was before there were all these accessible cell phones. The rule was that I would have to call my parents when I got somewhere and when I was in for the night. I never fought them on this. I knew I was their only child, and I knew how much I meant to them. I respected my mom and dad even in those sinful days, and I did as much as I could to give them some peace.

My mom and dad would often stay up all night praying for me; I knew they were beating on God's heavenly door for me, and they did that for years. My mom and dad's prayers were like German Shepherds on my tail. During all those years, they saw no fruit whatsoever; I went to church out of guilt even sometimes going still high on drugs. Still, as I sat there Sunday after Sunday, the gospel was being deposited into my soul, slowly but surely sweeping the dirt out the way.

I don't want to make it sound so hopeless. I was convicted many times; I went on youth trips and to youth camps during all those years. I made professions of faith because I was emotionally stirred. I walked the aisles many times and was baptized quite a bit; I would go down a dry sinner and come up a wet one. As I got older, I still maintained my sinful ways;

I was a very committed and faithful sinner. I give everything I do my all, and in this case, it was sin. If I was going to serve myself and sin, then I would give it all I had and indulge. If I was going to serve God, then I would do that with all that is in me. I was so miserable during this time straddling the fences. This is what the Prophet Elijah meant when he said, *"How long will you hesitate between two opinions? If the LORD is God, follow Him; but if Baal, follow him"(1 Kings 18:21 NASB).* I concur with him.

I look back now on the times my life was spared. There were times I turned down a ride home with someone only for them to get in a wreck with the passenger side of the car crushed. There were times I drove home with no idea how I got home. When I graduated high school and went to Cancun, Mexico, many things happened that could have ended in serious trouble, but God was merciful. I thank God for His plan and purpose. There are times when we are not aware of the devil's traps and without our knowledge God protects us and answers our prayers- even our unspoken ones.

Satan has plans, and they are plans of destruction; as the Bible says, "*Be of sober spirit, be on the alert. Your adversary, the devil, prowls around like a roaring lion, seeking someone to devour" (1 Peter 5:8 NASB).* God protects us from those plans. We also have our own plans. The Bible says "*The mind of man plans his way, But the LORD directs his steps" (Proverbs 16:9 NASB).* Most importantly, God has His plans; in fact the Scripture says, "*For I know the plans that I have for you,' declares the LORD, 'plans for welfare and not for calamity to give you a future and a hope.*

Then you will call upon Me and come and pray to Me, and I will listen to you. You will seek Me and find Me when you search for Me with all your heart'" (Jeremiah 29:11-13 NASB). That truth would resonate through my disappointments because it showed me that even when we pray, God's plan and purpose will prevail in spite of what we desperately want. Additionally, His plan and purpose will prevail in spite of Satan's plan to destroy us. God is in charge; we need to hear it and believe it. If Satan could kill us, he would have done it a long time ago.

After graduation, I moved out of my parent's house and into Lafayette which is about thirty minutes from New Iberia. During that time, I was attending the local university, working two jobs, going out every night, drinking every single day, and using drugs. My life was pretty full, and I could only take that kind of pressure for so long. I was going to college for performing arts, which branched out into directing and screenwriting for me. I really enjoyed character development, and it gave me an appreciation for writing. I also began to have the confidence to stand and to speak in front of people. Little did I know that God was training me for my destiny, one that I could not have seen.

TWO

My Salvation

"The people who were sitting in darkness saw a great light, and those who were sitting in the land and shadow of death, upon them a light dawned."
(Matthew 4:16 NASB)

"For God so loved the world that He gave His only begotten Son, that whoever believes in Him shall not perish, but have eternal life.
(John 3:16 NASB)

During my time in Lafayette, I moved a couple of times and lived with a couple of friends. I had one friend whom I reconnected with; he was older than I was and really used by God. When I went out with my friends, he was always there to drive me home or keep his eye out for me. He was the older brother I didn't have. Eventually in an attempt to slowly break away from the party environment that I was so accustomed to, I moved in with him. He always tried to encourage me and was a godly influence. I was able to slowly break away from the party environment, but the drinking still continued in private. During that period of my life, I knew that Satan was working overtime because the breakthrough was coming. The conviction of God was getting stronger and stronger as the weeks progressed. I can remember distinctly one night when I was drinking on my patio, and God told me that enough was enough. I told Him to leave me alone and stop convicting me. This came back to haunt me when Satan would later use this against me.

In October 1999, my mom and dad asked me to come to a revival meeting that their church was having, and I went. The guest pastor talked about the realities of being lost and dying without God, and while I had heard the gospel hundreds of time, this night would be different. He told the story of when he was by the bedside of his dying, cold-hearted grandfather; as he lay there dying, he began to sweat profusely and screamed, "Help me, help me!" He began to grip the sheets and rip them. The preacher said that it was truly a horrific sight, and it broke his heart. As I was listening, my heart began to pound because I remembered when I had told God to stop convincing me, and I was faced with the reality of my spiritual life. I knew enough about the Bible having heard so many sermons and having sat through many Bible studies to know that I was in a battle for my soul. It was as if every demon in hell were trying to cover my eyes and ears. I was certain my mom and dad's prayers were flooding heaven during that service. I now know what it is like to pray so hard that the scales come off of people's eyes. I thought of all the sleepless nights and all the faithfulness my mom and dad had shown to God. I can picture them crying out to God saying, "Please save our son tonight." My life was flashing before my eyes- my partying, my drinking, and my sinful lifestyle. It had taken its toll on me. I thought of all the years that I had made empty professions of emotional responses to God, and I was tired of doing that. The time had come when I had to make a decision. As I looked at God's mercy, it struck me that God had allowed me to live in rebellion to Him and His ways for twenty years. Throughout those years, I had lived in direct opposition to Him; I had come into His house still high from the night before and sat under the gospel, but in His mercy He was still gracious and long suffering. Finally, I had come to see that salvation was an extraordinary gift- a gift that I didn't deserve, yet a gift that is freely given. I also knew it was impossible for me to be saved and stay in the company of my friends. This was hard because I had enjoyed their company for so many years, but I knew I personally couldn't have both. I asked myself, "Am I ready to serve God whole heartedly?" Still Satan battled against God, and in a last ditch effort, he taunted me, "Kelly, God will never accept you; you blasphemed the Holy Spirit." The preacher then told the congregation how Jesus had come to save us from eternal damnation, and the light bulb went off and my soul was awakened. That verse about light coming into darkness came alive in my heart, and I was experiencing it. I came out of that fog of religion, and God instantly became my heart's desire. I could not wait to walk down that aisle that I had walked down all my teenage years, and when he said to come forward, I did. I leaned down on the side of the first pew and wept because for once I saw what a reproach I was to a holy God. It started to crystallize to me how I had abused His grace, how I trampled the blood of Jesus by my actions and thoughts. I realized how God had spared my life repeatedly all these years. When we finally walk into His glorious light, we see Him as He is, and we see ourselves as we are. I told God that I may have committed the unpardonable sin, but I would serve Him anyway. It was bittersweet because I rose from that moment changed, joyful, and relieved, but because I didn't know what blasphemy was, I felt condemned by Satan's words as I remembered that night I had told God to leave me alone. It wouldn't be until nearly a year later that I would come to understand what blasphemy was and that I hadn't committed it- another lie of Satan. Blasphemy is not telling God to leave us alone or to stop convicting us. Blasphemy is to resist or to deny the Holy Spirit; it is to remain in unbelief. For example, the Pharisees attributed the miracles of Jesus to the power of Satan even though they knew it was the power of God; this was blasphemy. Satan used that lie as long as he could. I am an avid studier of God's word, and I love to talk to people about hard things like that because I never want to see someone being tormented by something they don't understand. Going back to that night, I know it brought great joy to my parents because God had finally answered their prayer. I had been lost, but now I was a new creation in Christ Jesus.

The people who grow up in church repeatedly hearing the

gospel are often the hardest group to reach because they have heard it all many times and have grown callus to its power. I think of Uzzah in 2 Samuel. The Ark of the Covenant, which was holy and which represented God's presence, resided in the house of his father Abinadab. As Abinadab's son, Uzzah had grown up around the Ark and was too familiar with the Ark and disregarded the teaching in the Old Testament book of Numbers. The Ark was not to be touched (Numbers 4:15); however, Uzzah disobeyed this law when he "*reached out toward the ark of God and took hold of it, for the oxen nearly upset it. And the anger of the LORD burned against Uzzah, and God struck him down there for his irreverence; and he died there by the ark of God" (2 Samuel 6:6-7 NASB).* Familiarity had probably breed complacency, and even though I am sure he meant to protect the Ark, he forgot that he was to treat the Ark as the holy presence of God and obey God's command. I am afraid in some cases when kids grow up in church they become familiar with the presence of God and sometimes forgot the holiness and power of it. In my situation, this at least was true.

I went home that night a changed man. I also knew that the battle was only just beginning. Getting saved does not save us from our battles, but it does fill us with the grace and empowerment of the Lord. As a new Christian, some battles may immediately cease, but others may be left for us to continue the fight. Shortly after getting saved, I stopped going out to parties and bars with my friends because I no longer saw those things the same way and did not derive the same pleasure from them. I had a new nature- a divine nature; the Holy Spirit was living on the inside of me, convicting me, and this time I was listening and actually wanted to obey. The battle I continued to fight was drinking and smoking. Even though I still fought some battles, I was also reading my Bible and understanding it. My friend who had been a godly example in the last few years still continued to help me, but this time we were on the same page. He really encouraged me to not go out anymore, and I stopped. I went from hanging out with all of my friends to dropping off the map so to speak. I was still going to college, but even in that I had lost my desire. I loved acting and writing, but I really felt I wasn't going to pursue that much longer.

During this time, I began to look at the book of Revelation again to discover what these beasts were and the answers to other unanswered questions. Drawing on my love of the performing arts and remembering the outdated 1970's movie I had seen on the rapture, I decided that I wanted to write a screenplay about the end times. I involved my roommate and that filled many empty nights. As we began to work on that, I fell in love with the Word of God. I was still battling drinking at that time, but I asked God to take away the desire I had for drinking and smoking and to replace it with a hunger for Him and His word. At that time my insatiable hunger for reading was born. God also answered my prayer because the desires to drink and smoke left. We worked on that screenplay for months, and I learned so much during that time. I remember one day I was writing a scene that took place in Israel, but I had no clue what Israel looked like.

Sometimes when we are first saved it seems as if God answers every prayer immediately. One day soon after having this desire to see Israel, I was outside praying, and I asked God if there was any way possible that I could go to Israel to scout it out. You may think I am crazy, but I will never forget what I am about to tell you. As I prayed that simple prayer, a dove came and landed on a power line right above my head, and it looked right back at me. This gave me the chills as I remembered reading about the dove in the Bible. As I stood there, I felt that it was very possible that this would become a reality. My friend and I never finished our screenplay, but God was not finished with my desire to travel to Israel.

During this time Jeremy, one of my childhood friends, came for a visit. He was also was very interested in the things of the Lord, and as I began to tell him about my experience, he gave his life to the Lord. As my pastor today always says, "When you get saved, you only really need that one friend to be there with you in the beginning of your walk." I was blessed with a couple of them. My childhood friend was there, and we enjoyed many adventures as new Christians. It wasn't long after this that my life transitioned from Lafayette back to New Iberia. My time in Lafayette had come to an end, and I knew the Lord was leading me back home. My Lafayette roommate and I have lost touch, but he will always have a special place in my heart for being such a mighty inspiration at the beginning of my journey.

Once I was back in New Iberia, I attended a youth event that was very mission minded, and during this massive youth gathering, they gave an invitation to go on a month long mission trip. That night I went to the meeting, grabbed the information I needed, and was shocked to see the word "Israel." It was as if that word was lit up on the page, and I remembered that day with the dove. I went home and showed my mom and dad, and they were supportive as usual. The cost was $4,000 for the month-long trip. I didn't have that kind of money and neither did my parents. After moving back home, I had still continued to work in Lafayette at a giant electronic store. The next day I walked into work and asked my boss who was a Christian if he would give me off of work to take the trip, and he said he would. During that time, I learned a lot about walking in faith because God was opening doors that allowed me to go. Because neither my parents nor I had the money, we had to raise it ourselves. We washed cars and sold plate lunches to raise money. I can remember one time in particular when God performed a miracle of the loaves and fishes. For this particular fundraiser, we had cooked spaghetti and were selling plates of it. As we were serving, it looked like we were getting lower on food while there was still a line, but we kept serving the same amount on each plate, and it lasted until the last kid took his plate.

Can you remember the things God has done in your life? I want to encourage you to reflect on those times when you saw the Lord come through for you. Recall the mighty deeds He has done for you. Here I was having been saved for only a little over six months, and I was heading to the mission field. I was so excited because I had experienced God in a real tangible way. The groundwork of putting in the effort really paid off because I saw God move on the little faith I had.

I will never forget boarding that plane as I waved goodbye to my mom and dad. Of course they were petrified due to all of the Middle East turmoil that had been building. In the months before I left, the tension had begun to build between the Muslims and the Jews. It was very interesting to see it die down right before I left to go on the trip; I know that was an answered prayer for my mom and dad. I waved goodbye- and yes, we waved for a while like the old days. That day I flew to a missions training facility for the organization I was traveling with. I am a shy individual, and I was going to a place where I knew no one. However, God was preparing me for my calling because one day I would need that skill of meeting people in ministry. I arrived in Texas, and here I learned how to present the gospel to Jewish people, as well as Muslims. While the training was intense, it was a great experience.

From there we flew to Tel Aviv, Israel where we stayed for two weeks followed by two weeks in Jericho. We walked the same streets my Lord walked, and this trip further cemented my faith. I saw the Bible come alive, and even had the privilege of leading a Muslim to the Lord. After he had accepted Christ, he said, "My dad is a devout Muslim, and this decision will cost me everything." After returning home, I wrote to him and sent him some Worship CDs, but I heard nothing nor did I receive anything back. This has stayed with me for all of these years.

During our time in Jericho, we did an outreach using dramas and a Gospel presentation. As we began the drama, the park started filling up; our contact had favor in that community so he had set it all up. Jericho is predominately Muslim so we were in dangerous territory already. When our contact got up to present the gospel message, a Muslim high priest came into the crowd and started arguing with him. Then before we understood what was happening, the crowd started chanting something in Arabic, Palestinian flags came up, and members of the crowd started waving them. Armed guards moved into the crowd. This was a terrifying scene to us as young Christians, but God had given our contact a boldness I had never seen in action before. He stood toe to toe with this Muslim high priest and said, "The Lord rebuke you. We have permission to be here, and we will finish presenting this gospel no matter what." The Lord honored that step of faith because the priest backed down, the crowed hushed, and the armed guards faded into the background. I would learn later that the group was the same Hamas group you hear about on the news. I would love to say I remember thousands getting saved, but I honestly have to say all I remember after that presentation was getting on our bus and rocks being thrown at it.

We still had a week there, and we walked those streets in holy boldness. Some of the Muslims would get on the loud speaker and say things against us while we were there walking the streets evangelizing the same streets the biblical Patriarch Joshua had walked. The locals told others to stay away from the Americans because we had prostitutes with us, but we just kept our eyes on the mission. God was so amazing on those streets that week. We would pray specific prayers to the Lord; we would ask God to send us divine appointments asking such things as, "Lord send us three guys with a red shirt, a blue shirt and a yellow shirt." And He would! During those weeks, I saw the gospel come alive, especially the Scripture that says,

"Greater is He that is in you than he who is in the world" (1 John 4:4 NASB). The trip didn't produce a lot of salvations, but we planted a lot of seeds.

While in Israel, I was baptized in the Jordan River. Though I had been in the baptismal countless times during all those years of emotional experiences, this time it truly meant something to me. I knew that I had finally surrendered. We were also able to spend some time in the Garden of Gethsemane, and it forever changed the way I see Jesus's agonizing night in the garden. We had ministered late into the night and had to get up early for a tour the next morning. Our leader taught us, and then we went into the garden to have our quiet time. I found a spot under one of those giant olive trees and opened my Bible to that account, but as I started reading, I fell asleep! The next thing I remember was being awakened by a fellow missionary, and I realized what had happened. I felt horrible! I realized I had wasted a once in a lifetime opportunity, and to add insult to injury, as we were walking out I saw a plaque on the wall outside the garden that asked, "Could you not stay awake for one hour?" This may sound humorous to some, but I now have a soft spot for the disciples who fell asleep.

After the trip was over, we returned to Texas for debriefing. As I landed back on American soil, I knew I was forever changed. My faith had become more firm as I had seen God do so many things in my life during this month. I had seen the Bible come to life, and I had experienced persecution for my faith. I felt like Polycarp (an early church martyr who was burned at the stake for his faith), well not really. When I returned home to

Louisiana and I told my mom and dad all that had happened, I know it blessed them once again to see God answer their prayer as He was growing me. I remember vividly the night I returned home and lay in the bedroom I had grown up in. I looked around at those walls that I had looked at for years; those walls and that ceiling would be the last things I saw when I came in from nights spent partying. Then I would lie down full of guilt and worry night after night about what I had put inside my body, but this time I lay in that bed changed forever. I was at peace reflecting on all God had spared me from and what He allowed me to experience in the land of the Bible. My heart was so full all I could do was cry for what seemed like hours in gratitude for the Lord's presence in my life. I was a fireball of excitement, and my desire to be used by God was growing more and more.

When I went back to church, my pastor at that time asked me to preach and give a testimony about the trip. I was scared, but I agreed. After I'd preached my first sermon, it wasn't long before I was told I had a call on my life, and I felt something that I had never felt before. I knew it was a calling because I couldn't explain it. Anyone who has ever had a call on their life to preach the gospel says the same thing. It is unexplainable, not as a matter of pride, but it becomes a weight- a burden- that you carry. It is something that no job or amount of money can satisfy; no matter how successful you become at any other job, ministry is all you think about. I didn't know then what capacity this calling would be in; I just knew I had this unquenchable desire to serve God, and it was never filled when

I was working at another job. I am not driven by money; I am driven by purpose. The number one goal I have is to serve God and fulfill His purpose in my life for His kingdom at any cost, but sometimes you receive the calling, long before you are in a position to be in full time ministry.

Allow me to break from the story and say this before I go forward, and that is we lose many young Christians when they are called to preach the gospel early in their walk with the Lord; their identity becomes rooted in the call and not in their relationship with God. If the opportunities do not come quickly enough, discouragement can occur as they form a distrust of spiritual authority, God, or a word spoken over them. They can close their eyes to any other purpose or plan or process God will use to develop them. In the beginning, God's presence is often felt in a real and tangible way, and it seems as if God is answering every prayer, and we unknowingly put our faith in all of these feelings. As the Christian experience continues, there are periods of time when God begins to teach us about walking in faith, times when He seems silent, and when prayers seem to go unanswered. It's a place where we feel we are in the desert and His presence is absent. During these times Christians will either develop an even greater thirst for God, or they give up waiting and die from exhaustion. When a child first begins to walk parents hold them with both hands and guide them, but how would it look if the parents were still doing that at five or ten years old? How would it look if you still slept in your parents' bed when you are fifteen years old? How would it look if you saw a teenager with a pacifier in his mouth? (However, during the rave days in the 1990's I saw that quite a bit.) What I'm trying to say is growth must happen, and it happens as God drops our hands and steps back letting us walk on our own. Then he will go into another room and wait for us to come to him; he is training us to follow His voice. As we get older, we begin to stay at home by ourselves, and we gain more responsibility and more training because ultimately the goal is not comfort but action. In the world, growing up is about learning independence; in God's kingdom, it is about growing in dependence. This can only come by growing in faith when we cannot see or hear. God's desire is that we grow in His purpose for our lives, and He creates situations that lead to this.

Luke relays the same principle as he says, "*Now large crowds were going along with Him; and He turned and said to them, 'If anyone comes to Me, and does not hate his own father and mother and wife and children and brothers and sisters, yes, and even his own life, he cannot be My disciple. Whoever does not carry his own cross and come after Me cannot be My disciple. For which one of you, when he wants to build a tower, does not first sit down and calculate the cost to see if he has enough to complete it? Otherwise, when he has laid a foundation and is not able to finish, all who observe it begin to ridicule him, saying, 'This man began to build and was not able to finish. Or what king, when he sets out to meet another king in battle, will not first sit down and consider whether he is strong enough with ten thousand men to encounter the one coming against him with twenty thousand? Or else, while the other is still far away, he sends a delegation and asks for terms of peace. So then, none of you can be My disciple who does not give up all his own possessions""* *(Luke 14:25-33 NASB).* There are always the large crowds walking after Him who will not finish the race because they have not considered the cost; they gather just because there is a crowd. At the same time Jesus was not advocating that we abandon our families. He simply meant that we should not prefer anything over Him. Afterwards, He says that we should carry our cross and count the cost. There is a cost that comes with following Him; simply put, some things will not go like we think it should because we now have to change our focus to what furthers His kingdom and not ours.

Laying the foundation is easy, but building the structure is hard- sometimes the funds run low. I can say this from my own experience; initially, the building plans did not meet my expectations and that is where I crumbled. Christianity is not how we begin, but how He builds. We want to be the architect and the builder, but that is not following Jesus. That is conditional love and discipleship. Jesus is saying we must give Him all that we are, all we desire, and all that we will be. Jesus never hid this fact. He told this very thing to the rich young ruler, and while his cousin, John the Baptist, was in prison, he said, *"Blessed is he, whosoever shall not be offended in me." (Matthew 11: 6 KJV).* Looking back, Jesus was telling me basically the same thing. I should not get offended at him when it doesn't go like I expected. The cost of following Jesus is great, but the reward is greater.

Ponder on this: What if your greatest desire was not fulfilled or your greatest prayer not answered? What if the reason is because God wanted one person to see that, and as a result of them watching your faith, they come to know Him. Let's say you lose a child- the greatest desire of your heart. As a result, a young mother who has taken her own child for granted views your circumstance, and it completely changes her view on how she should cherish the gift God has given her. As a result of your circumstance, that same mother sees you rise up in your faith in spite of your loss. You still choose to believe God is good and sovereign no matter what happened, and she sees you glorify God even if you don't understand why. That young mother may be so moved that she gives her life to the Lord, and she deepens the relationship she has with her child. Would you say, "Lord, here is my child use this for your glory" prior to knowing what is coming? No, you would stop that child and not allow them to leave the house. I believe that is the honest human response. However, God sees things differently, and His ways are not our ways, and His thoughts are not our thoughts. God may not cause that to happen, but because He has foreknowledge and because He is sovereign and all knowing, He can use the situation for His glory and for the good of those who are called according to His purpose. We exchange our cost for His cost, our way for His way. Ultimately everything in our lives must come through the fingers of God, good or bad. He is never mindless or caught off guard by a situation or circumstance in our lives.

As I began to adjust back to life in New Iberia I had stayed in contact with my childhood friend Jeremy. We had many adventures in our desire to change the world starting in New

Iberia, Louisiana. He knew someone from another church who seemed kind of "out there." Jeremy had arranged a great witnessing opportunity to go and reach the world- well, actually a little trailer in a small trailer park. Our first experience on this mission field was witnessing to a man living in this trailer park. We sat around his kitchen table studying our Bibles together, and though we had gone to witness to him, after about an hour into the conversation, Jeremy and I felt lost like we were the ones who needed Jesus. He said we needed to be baptized in Jesus's name only, and if we had been baptized in the name of the Father, Son, and Holy Spirit, then we were not saved. He also said that we should be able to speak in tongues right after that experience according to Acts 2:38. He had made such a compelling case that we literally felt lost. He then proceeded to tell us that we could get baptized that night, and all of our fears would go away.

He called the leaders of his church to quickly go unlock the doors of the church telling them he was bringing some men who desperately needed the Lord. He told us to follow him, and as we were walking to our cars, he stressed in the most serious tone, "I want you to follow my vehicle closely, and whatever you do, don't wreck before you get into the baptismal tank." He was implying we would die lost. At this point, Jeremy and I were petrified, but we had one goal in life at this point- not to wreck! We followed in silence at a close distance. The ride seemed to take days. We arrived and were greeted by two men at the door of the church who gave us a heartfelt welcome. We entered the church, and it was dark with small embers of light.

As we adjusted our eyes, we saw men in white shirts lined up against the walls of the church. We were lead up to an altar which looked like a big wooden block of some sort. We were told to get on our knees and cry out to God, and we did. We were deep in prayer, partially because we wanted to experience the baptism with Holy Spirit, but also because we were afraid for our lives. As we were crying out to God with our heads down, a man approached us beating on this giant wooden block next to us and he proceeded to scream in our ears asking us if we really wanted it. At this point the "it" could have been a number of things- death, torture, safety, sanity- but in our minds, the "it" was the Holy Spirit or a way out of there. After a long time, they thought either we were ready or so fearful that we would try to escape, and Jeremy and I found ourselves in a back room holding two white robes. We were told to take off our clothes and put them on. I couldn't help but think of that show from the 1970's that I had seen about the book of Revelation where they had to put on white robes before they approached a guillotine to be executed because they would not take the mark of the beast. We walked out of that closet, and I went first. I was led into a tank of warm water. It was the kind of tank I had been in countless times through all my emotional experiences with God. Before this, I had been baptized in the Jordan River, and that was the baptism I count as my real water baptism because I was saved before that trip. I had also been baptized in the Holy Spirit in a little Messianic Church in Israel where I fell and got up speaking in other tongues. However, according to this guy, this was supposed to happen all at one time. Needless to say he put me under the water and baptized me in the name of Jesus only, and I came out with no new desire or utterance. He tried to coach me in saying, "Lalalalalal," but to no avail. So he gave up on me and tossed me to the side and led Jeremy in. The same experience happened to him. We were told to go back and put our clothes back on and not to give up. At this point I was just happy that there was no guillotine, and we were still alive. They were kind though, and they led us into this kitchen area where they gave us some Kool-Aid and cookies. (I know what you are thinking about the Kool-Aid; it was cherry.) We ended the conversation by answering some questions, one of them being what size shirt we wore. We simply thanked them for taking their time to help us and for their hospitality. Jeremy and I got in his Camaro and drove off speedily unlike our slow pace driving there. We went through a couple of other experiences like this.

There was another time when a traveling evangelist came through town; he was from a denomination that could be found in the cult section at bookstores - and yes, that was from his mouth. He had come through doing a prophecy convention, and Jeremy and I were interested. We met every night in a hotel for about three weeks until he informed us that his lease had run out, and he had to move the conference to a particular church in town. Jeremy and I thought, "Well, we stuck it out this long; let's go." During these weeks, we had come to know the evangelist well, and he proceeded to tell us that the church was having some problems with the pastor and that the members wanted him out. He felt like the Lord wanted us to be co-pastors of that church. He gave us a tour and said the services meet on Saturdays. Then he began to tell us their doctrine, and we knew this was not for us. Jeremy and I continued to go to the conference, but it soon became more about getting people to join that church than prophecy. By this time we had checked out mentally, but we were still going because we felt bad for the evangelist. He really was a genuine person who loved God and that really spoke to me. The last I heard, he is still traveling the country.

In Christianity, there are so many doctrinal issues, and my intention is not to try to prove one over the other. However, I will say that there are some fundamental beliefs that have no wiggle room. My point in telling these stories is that they taught me to dig for myself. From early in my walk, these types of things grew my desire for truth, and I learned not to lean on just what a man says. It would be sometime in the future that I would have to search for God's goodness in suffering. God was preparing me to push through and embrace Him and trust. He was using all these experiences to train and teach me; these are things I didn't know I needed, but these things would prove to be vital on my journey. I would go to church every time the doors were opened it seemed, and God was teaching me so many things. My pastor at the time would tell me that he felt that I would be in ministry one day although I didn't know what that meant or really looked like at that point. I just knew I had an unquenchable fire that was burning outside of my fireplace.

THREE

Growing Pains

The godly may trip seven times, but they will get up again.
(Proverbs 24:16 NLT)

In time, I really began to grow in my faith. I had gotten saved in October of 1999 and was on the mission field the following summer. The more I did for the Lord, the hungrier I grew. I must say that during this infant stage of salvation, I think I took on too much. When I say that, I mean I went too deep too fast. When someone comes to the Lord their appetite is insatiable, but meat should never be given to those who need milk. Because I had gone to church for so long in my lost state, I felt that I was behind in my growth; there is a difference between sitting in church for years and growing in God. Before we come to Christ, we are dead and our souls are dead in our sin. This point is supported by the Apostle Paul: "*And you were dead in your trespasses and sins, in which you formerly walked according to the course of this world, according to the prince of the power of the air, of the spirit that is now working in the sons of disobedience. Among them we too all formerly lived in the lusts of our flesh, indulging the desires of the flesh and of the mind, and were by nature children of wrath, even as the rest. But God, being rich in mercy, because of His great love with which He loved us, even when we were dead in our transgressions, made us alive together with Christ (by grace you have been saved), and raised us up with Him, and seated us with Him in the heavenly places in Christ Jesus" (Ephesians 2:1-6 NASB).* Paul is telling us that before Christ comes into our lives we are dead to His ways. We have scales on our eyes so to speak. All we know as human beings is to function in every capacity under the domination of our flesh. Paul would again buttress this point in his letter to the Corinthians: "*But a natural man does not accept the things of the Spirit of God, for they are foolishness to him; and he cannot understand them, because they are spiritually appraised" (1 Corinthians 2:14 NASB).*

Jesus also spoke specifically to this point in the story of Nicodemus found in John's Gospel: "*Now there was a man of the Pharisees, named Nicodemus, a ruler of the Jews; this man came to Jesus by night and said to Him, 'Rabbi, we know that You have come from God as a teacher; for no one can do these signs that You do unless God is with him.' Jesus answered and said to him, 'Truly, truly, I say to you, unless one is born again he cannot see the kingdom of God'" (John 3:1-3 NASB).* We always take this to mean that man cannot see heaven, but He did not say the "kingdom of heaven." He was speaking about the kingdom of God that functions on earth as it does in heaven. The kingdom of God is the ways and things of God that function here on this earth. For example, sowing and reaping is a principle of the kingdom of God. Tithing to the local church is a kingdom principle. Loving our enemies instead of fighting them is a spiritual principle. God's word is the standard of His kingdom and His principles were made to function in our earthly realm as it already does in heaven. I say all of that to say that before we come to know Jesus as Lord, we simply cannot understand the things of God as we should because we are spiritually dead. When Adam fell in the garden, he plummeted the whole human race into spiritual death. Our eyes were darkened, so sitting in a church building will not awaken our spirits until the one who established and built that institution comes in and awakens our souls and spirits. When we pray for someone who is lost, we pray that their soul and spirit come alive. For when they do, they will be "*dead to sin, but alive to God in Christ Jesus*" *(Romans 6:11 NASB).*

At the great exchange, when Christ bore our sin upon Himself at the cross and we inherited His righteousness, He redeemed what we lost at the fall. When we have been awakened by the Spirit of God, we have a new identity in Christ and the sinful lives we lived before are now dead. We are to reckon ourselves, which is an accounting term that is used to describe the need to align what we see with what the Word of God says. Again the Apostle Paul teaches us, "*Or do you not know that all of us who have been baptized into Christ Jesus have been baptized into His death? Therefore we have been buried with Him through baptism into death, so that as Christ was raised from the dead through the glory of the Father, so we too might walk in newness of life. For if we have become united with Him in the likeness of His death, certainly we shall also be in the likeness of His resurrection, knowing this, that our old self was crucified with Him, in order that our body of sin might be done away with, so that we would no longer be slaves to sin; for he who has died is freed from sin" (Romans 6:3-7 NASB).* The word "baptism" can be used literally or figuratively. Figuratively speaking, we are raised to walk as Christ walked, meaning we are a new creature made to walk in His ways. I have said all of this to say that I had sat in church spiritually asleep to the things of God; however, I was blind to how much I had missed, and mistakenly believed I should be doing more because I had been a church-goer for so long. I have seen in my life that people rush to tell a new convert that they have a call on their life; generally speaking, people take that to mean that they will be a pastor who shepherds a church or an evangelist who will speak to thousands. Many will then put their identity in a calling instead of Christ, and then they monitor everything they do with the motive of "The Calling." I know this from experience.

Early in my walk, I was told by people in authority that I had a calling and one day I would be a pastor. I must say it was a tremendous honor to hear that because everyone wants to be valued, and everyone wants to do something big for God and have influence for the kingdom of God, but what is not told is that it comes with a tremendous price. I was told this many times through people who didn't even know each other. I will never forget one such man and one of the greatest men of God I have ever met, Heath who was my project director and who to this day I think about all the time. I am grateful that God allowed me to spend a month in Israel with him, and during this time, he modeled great leadership qualities and inspired me greatly. While I was in Israel, the Holy Spirit placed His desire on the inside of me, and I felt that calling and desire for ministry began to grow. When there is something the Lord has for you to do, He will also give you the desire and a burden for it. Let's be clear on something- a man does not own the anointing or can distribute a call to ministry. That great power belongs to the Lord, and it is distributed by the Holy Spirit of God. A man can only recognize the call on his life and confirm what is there. I heard a well-known preacher say that people come to him during altar calls and ask him for his anointing. He said that he then prays for trials, suffering, and sleepless nights with burdens before they say, "Stop, Preacher." He then tells them, "Well, you want the anointing; that comes in the fire of adversity." That spoke volumes to me as I look back on what I have experienced.

There were so many things that happened during this early time in my walk, but I will highlight only one. I was a relatively young Christian at this time. My pastor at that time called me in his office and told me that a nearby church had called and was looking for a youth pastor. He asked if I was interested, and he believed this would be a great opportunity to get my feet wet, so to speak. At the time, I had a full time job, but working in ministry was my second greatest desire next to having children so I took the position. I was now working in ministry which was everything I had always desired, and I would love to tell you that I was thriving and going great, but I would be lying to you. I did not have a good experience. For the first time, I saw ministry and was very shaken by the isolation I felt in the spiritual realm of it. To make a long story short, my ministry experience ended in total discouragement. It was just too much for me too early. Although to be honest, I did learn about what not to do in ministry. As I walked away from failure in ministry, I wondered if I had missed God. I became bitter and hurt because of my experiences.

During this time, I experienced pain of failure on a grander scale than ever before. There were other things in addition to my experience in ministry that took a toll on me which resulted in heartbreak. This pain was all happening at once, and I felt like failure had made me an outcast. I felt like I was a second-class Christian. I felt like I had ruined everything by some of the choices I had made. This felt much like when I was first saved, and I had thought I had committed blasphemy. Still, I was determined to serve God even if; I felt like a spiritual cripple though I continued to preserve.

In an effort to do this, I went back on the mission field; this time to Peru. When I was on the mission field, it did great things for me; I was able to truly empty myself on foreign soil, and missions really catapulted my faith beyond the basic. Peru was a trip of fruitfulness; there were many salvations and supernatural healings that took place, and it gave me a chance to escape the pain I was going through. This trip taught me how to push through in adversity, and how to serve despite my personal feelings. This would become tremendously important because of what was coming down the road. I can remember being on that trip and those thoughts of failure would try to creep in as I would just stare into the heavens feeling hopeless; I wanted to do more for God. I had taken on the identity of my disappointments. However, in the midst of these, I would then witness God do great things, like healing a lady who was crippled in front of my eyes.

This occurred in a small town village outside of Lima, Peru. We went into this town and invited the entire village to come and see our drama which was a tremendous visual of the gospel; many decisions were made for Christ due to the presentation. This particular time, we presented the drama and gave the altar call. Many people responded including this one lady who walked up on crutches. There was a person on each side guiding her because even with the crutches her legs were so bowed backwards. When we bend our knees, they bend in front of us, but her knees bent toward the back instead of the front. A group of us gathered around her and began to pray. As I looked around, tears were rolling down everyone's cheeks. She began weeping, and we backed away as she gave her crutches to someone and began walking. The town was mesmerized because they all knew her condition. We had experienced a miracle! We held a crusade that night, and she came up and testified. We had a wonderful service where people came and gave their lives to Jesus. This trip exposed me to the supernatural power of God, and I walked away from that trip with a renewed hope. I still felt tarnished, but I was healing slowly; however, when I came back to the United States and my reality, I still felt crippled.

It was during this time that my Dad and I stepped out in faith by starting a lawn service, and it was great. We were able to work together for ourselves. We started out by cutting small yards, and the Lord was providing tremendously for us and our business began to grow. The greatest thing about this job was working with my dad every day, and my mom would also cut on the weekends with us; it was truly a family business. Things were looking up for us. During this time, the Lord blessed us with a contract that gave us stability and really kept us busy. It was great because this meant more time to sit on the lawn mower and feed myself for eight to ten hours a day listening to biblical messages and teachings. I guess you can say it was really like attending bible college! All that I was learning was sticking in my spirit because I was so hungry for God's word and cutting grass was not a job but a desk to learn under the open heavens. My dad and I had many talks during this time that helped both of us to grow in our faith. Before we got that contract, we would clean and paint tombstones for different families in the area. We always said how great it would be if the Lord would return for the rapture of the Church while we were cleaning the tombs. Conversations like these will always stay in my heart.

Some time would pass, and my life would change forever in a good way. There was a particular tire shop in town where I went to have my oil changed and for maintenance on the lawn mowers. It was at this shop that I would meet my wife. Over a period of time, I got to know the secretary at the tire shop, Shannon. One day my dad and I took off and went crabbing. I remember so vividly we caught ninety crabs in less than an hour! I was never the kind of guy who liked to initiate a date, but this time I guess I was feeling a little brave. I called and invited Shannon to come to our crab boil. She accepted and brought her ten-year-old son Dylan. We all hit it off immediately. From what I remember, he and I threw the baseball the whole time. From that day, we began dating, and the rest became our history.

It is funny how God works in our lives. One of my good friends from high school was a guy named Sean, and we did a lot of bad things together in the world. He had an older sister named Shannon, who I had never met because she had moved out by the time Sean and I became friends. Shannon had always said she would never date any of Sean's friends because they were trouble. She knew my name, but fortunately she had never met me, so technically I guess my association with Sean didn't count.

I will never forget a conversation Shannon and I had while we were sitting at the dining room table some time later. We began to talk about a possible future because the relationship was getting serious. I asked Shannon about having children because I wanted to lay my desire on the table. She said that she wasn't sure if she wanted more kids, but she did say she wanted to take time to see how I was with Dylan which was very wise, and I completely understood. She said that once she was comfortable with my relationship with Dylan, then she would feel comfortable with us having children. I will get back to this a little later. Dylan and I's relationship has been wonderful. I can truly say I see him as my own blood. Shannon and I married on

November 19, 2005, and it was beautiful service. My dad sang a beautiful song from a parents' point of view about watching their children grow up and starting their own family. I collected footage from our childhoods and made a video to go along with the song. It touched both of our families. My life seemed to be going perfectly. The storms clouds of my past were blown away, and it looked like sunshine in the future.

FOUR

The Boat Named Cancer

And those in the boat worshiped him, saying,
"Truly you are the Son of God."
(Matthew 14:33 ESV)

Life was going great. I was doing what I loved. I was married and had a wonderful son. We had moved into the trailer Shannon had so we could save money and buy a house. I had been renting during this time, and we wanted a place of our own. I had what I had always wanted. I had no idea what was coming, and I was not prepared at all. My dad had been passing blood in his stool, but he had put off going to the doctor because our business was so busy. After months of bleeding, my dad went to the doctor, and our family doctor sent my dad to get a colonoscopy. My mom, dad and I went for the results, and I will never forget this day as long as I live. The doctor walked in and told us, "Larry, you have colon cancer. We need to operate immediately." I remember getting so weak and feeling like I had to throw up. I looked at my dad's face, and he was as white as a ghost. I could see his mind processing the diagnosis. I could see fear rising up, but he was also trying to be strong for my mom and me. This time he wasn't strong enough. My dad always had the right answer to say at a time of crisis, but this time words left him. I remember looking at my best friend, my dad, my coach, my sparring partner. The man who would sneak into my room as a child and wake me up after long working hours just to hold me close because he missed me and the best quarterback I had ever seen in a backyard football game was being crushed, and there was nothing I could do. It was like Superman had kryptonite growing on the inside of him. I saw my mom, and it looked as if she had been shot through the heart. The comforting words that she had always given our family went silent as fear gripped her throat. Her childhood sweetheart since 12-years-old had been given a devastating blow.

Instantly it seemed as if we were in a boat on the Sea of Galilee. The storm was raging, and the last person we thought of was Jesus. The doctor was talking, but I couldn't hear a thing. Anger rose up in my heart, and sadness overtook my whole being. We were paralyzed by fear and smothered with doubt and worry. The times that I saw Jesus multiply spaghetti and heal a lady right before my eyes were a distant memory. I thought, "I have to be strong for them," but I just couldn't. It was something I would need if I was ever going to pastor, but there was no way I could do this at that moment. We were all just trying to process this. Waves were coming over us, and we were losing our breath. We found ourselves afraid and hopeless in a battered boat. My dad was crushed, but he was more worried about my mom and me. The doctor assured us, "Larry, we are going to get this thing," Our lives were changed forever as we went back into the waiting room and just cried and held each other. As we looked into the future, all we could see was cancer, fear, and the real possibility of death. The drive home was silent. The scenery I had seen all my life growing up looked bland and dark. Any type of comfort or positive expectation was gone. Nothing felt the same. Nothing looked the same.

When we got home, the house we had lived in all my life seemed lifeless for the first time. I sat and looked around the house and would see flashes of life as it was lived in this house. My dad and I had made music videos with us dancing and singing in the kitchen. I looked in the kitchen and imagined that scene, but pain rose up instead of joy. I looked at the floor where my dad and I had wrestled, and now I wondered if the day would come when he couldn't even stand. I looked into the backyard where we had thrown the ball, and there was just cold, empty silence. My dad was sitting at the kitchen table crying and repenting that he had not sought God about this. His words were, "I can't believe I didn't look to God for comfort. I went straight to fear and doubt." It was true. All of us had just felt sadness, anger, and worry without ever seeking the Lord for comfort. We had never prayed about the diagnosis. We were not prepared at all. Storms reveal who we are and who God is to us. God is who He is no matter what happens in our lives, but what is revealed is how we view Him. I heard a preacher say that in the life of a Christian there are three places he will find himself. We are either about to go into a storm, currently in a storm, or coming out of one. The severity and time periods of the storms will differ, but they are there. Jesus said, *"And the rain fell, and the floods came, and the winds blew and beat on that house, but it did not fall, because it had been founded on the rock." (Matthew 7:25 ESV).* Jesus did not say, "If they come;" he said, "And the rain fell." The storms will come; the deciding factor is not the storm, but the foundation of the house. What is the house built on? Many build their house on the rock of Jesus, but the foundation is still faulty. For example, many believe that if they place their faith in Jesus Christ and build their house on His rock, then storms will not buffet them, and if there is a perceived storm, they should not "claim it" or accept it. Consider this: what if when Jesus asked people what He could do for them, they responded, "Nothing, Lord. I don't claim I have anything wrong." If they had not acknowledged their storm, they would not have received what they needed. You may have been told that once you are saved life will be great. You may have been told that money will come your way and Christianity will be smooth sailing with the wind always at your back. Technically, you have built your house on Christ, but the foundation of your faith is missing key ingredient, as well as truths. If you are told that storms come because you have a lack of faith, that belief eventually hardens into your foundation, and it will surely crack. Some people feel like the rich young ruler who said, "I do this, and I do that. I keep the commandments," and in the end, when the storms come, we walk away sorrowful and bitter. We feel as if they shouldn't visit our shores. I'm sorry to say that I did not understand this heading into these storms, and more storms were still to come.

In the midst of my dad's cancer, we had to change our perspective. Instead of focusing on the cancer, we had to focus on God's purpose, and this purpose was being revealed and achieved through my dad's experiences and his responses to the opportunities they presented. God was sustaining my dad in supernatural ways as we went further down the road. The doctor was amazed for a couple of reasons. First, my dad never lost his hair even after the doctor guaranteed him that he would lose it in the chemo chair as he took his first chemotherapy treatment. Overall, he would sit in that chair over eighty times to receive treatment and kept a head full of hair throughout. He would have side effects that would come upon him, but he always pushed through. He would also continue to work hard while undergoing chemo. The doctor also said that generally when cancer comes back a second time; it doesn't stay in one spot, but it travels. However, when my dad's would return, it always remained isolated to the liver. It was amazing the people we would run into at the doctor's visits. We prayed for other patients, the doctors, and even the nurses. When my dad would take chemo treatments, he and my mom would often minister to people and pray for their healing and strength. I went with him at times, and I saw my mom and dad praying with and encouraging patients facing a brand new diagnosis. Many would be in shock when they asked my dad how many treatments he had taken, and he would tell them it was in the eighties. They would all tell him that he didn't look like he even had cancer. Once again that was answered prayers for us because God knew it would be harder seeing him sick. At their church, he was still serving as a deacon and a worship leader. Many times, I saw my dad sick with the effects of the chemo on Saturday night, but when Sunday morning came, he was ready to lead worship. God's purpose in our lives will give us a reason to continue no matter what circumstances we are facing. This was something I learned from my dad that would be invaluable later. When we cut grass, we were cutting about 400 acres a month. My dad would leave the chemo chair and cut and trim with me in the Louisiana heat of July. He would stop to vomit and keep going. This would continue all day many times. My dad continued to move in faith serving God.

Jesus was giving grace in the sickness and was giving us strength and hope that we didn't have before. One day I was there and a Muslim man let me pray for his healing in the name of Jesus. Another time, we left the hospital after a treatment and stopped at a local gas station we often used for our lawn care business. We began talking to a lady who often worked the counter, and through small talk, the subject of sickness came up. My dad began to tell her what he was going through, and my dad's testimony inspired the lady to call over her friend who had a child in need of a serious heart operation. The child was only about 6-years-old, and as you can imagine was afraid. My dad and I laid hands on the child and compassion filled our hearts as we prayed for him by the beer cooler. We got word a couple of weeks later that the surgery had gone well. His mom gave us a picture of him that I have to this day. My dad showed me that tragedies give us opportunities to do exploits for God if we have eyes to see and ears to hear. I look at the story of the disciples, and the Lord spoke to my heart through this story and that changed my life forever.

Matthew's Gospel tells of an account when the disciples boarded a boat at the command of Jesus. Matthew reports, *"Immediately He made the disciples get into the boat and go ahead of Him to the other side, while He sent the crowds away. After He had sent the crowds away, He went up on the mountain by Himself to pray; and when it was evening, He was there alone. But the boat was already a long distance from the land, battered by the waves; for the wind was contrary. And in the fourth watch of the night He came to them, walking on the sea" (Matt 14:22-25 NASB).* The disciples followed the command of Jesus, and still the storm came. We see that storms come even while we are in the will of God, but we must stand on His promise. That is something the disciples lost sight of. Jesus had told them that they were going over to the other side, but in the storm, they forgot the promise and the destination. We also see from this account that storms can come up suddenly. Before the disciples knew what was happening, they were in a battle for their lives. For us, a negative report can come at any moment. We can go to bed one night and wake up to devastation, and all of a sudden life looks totally different. Sometimes all it takes is one phone call to say that your child has been in an accident. It can catch us by surprise, but it never catches the Lord off guard. Jesus knew where the disciples were just as he knows where we are in our storms. When Jesus went to rescue them, He knew where to find them because they were where He had told them to go. I have been on the Sea of Galilee, and it is a big wide lake. In a raging storm, there is no doubt that the boat was moved quite a distance from where they were expected to be, but then the Bible continues and says, *"When the disciples saw Him walking on the sea, they were terrified, and said, 'It is a ghost!' And they cried out in fear. But immediately Jesus spoke to them, saying, 'Take courage, it is I; do not be afraid'" (Matt 14:26-27 NASB).* One thing that I know for certain is that our storms and trials bring Jesus. Like I have heard one say, "The very thing that was about to destroy them, Jesus used as a sidewalk to deliver them." I have always heard it taught that the storm may be cancer, miscarriage, loss of a child, the loss of a job, or financial struggles; however, in this story and my dad's battle, I came to see by revelation that cancer was the boat that God was using in our storm. Jesus was using cancer to cement and grow our faith. Jesus was using cancer as a boat to house opportunities for my dad to minister to others. Cancer put us in places we routinely wouldn't have gone. Before this, we really had no reason to go to hospitals and chemo facilities, but once in this boat, we constantly found ourselves praying for people everywhere we went. The cancer diagnosis put compassion in our hearts for others dealing with sickness and loss. Remember the water that is over our head is still beneath Jesus's feet and the boat. God is the creator of the wind and the water so He is not bound by the natural. In fact all things are under his control. We began learning firsthand the importance of developing a faith like Peters: *"Peter said to Him, 'Lord, if it is You, command me to come to You on the water.'*

And He said, 'Come!' And Peter got out of the boat, and walked on the water and came toward Jesus" (Matt 14:28-29 NASB). Our ability to step outside of what we are in will empower us to walk on what the natural says we can't. It is not natural for someone who has cancer to pray for people who have cancer because many times they can't see past their own diagnosis, but the Lord is on the water saying, "Step out of what you are in, and come where I am." Peter couldn't walk on water whether it was calm or raging. Walking on water cannot be done until Jesus commands us to do so, but once commanded, we must step out of our normal. For some, cancer is the new normal. For others, loss is the new normal. Peter did not walk on the water as much as he walked on the command, "Come!" If we are listening in our boat, Jesus will call us to do the impossible, and if we step out, we will perform mighty exploits for Him.

Let me give you an example. My dad had to do blood work every two weeks and scans just about every two months. Those were our stormy times. We were in the boat of cancer which had become our new normal; and we would get so nervous waiting for the test results. We knew that a bad report could capsize us; however, it was in those times that we would step out and minister to those around us. In the PET scan rooms with our palms sweating and our hearts racing, we ministered and prayed with other people feeling the same things. This was us stepping out of our boat and doing the Lord's work. My mom and dad were there many times to pray for people who had received devastating news. Our ability to walk on water depends on where our focus is. If we focus on the boat, we will focus only on what is happening to us and what we think we can control. If we focus on the waves, we will only focus on what can destroy us and our boats, but if we keep our eyes on Jesus, we will be where He is and do what He does. Let's revisit the story of Peter as he walks on water towards Jesus's voice: *"But seeing the wind, he became frightened, and beginning to sink, he cried out, 'Lord, save me!'" (Matt 14:30 NASB).* Did the water sink him? Did the wind stop him? No, he began to sink because he took his eyes off of Jesus who was not affected by the storm. The Bible continues, *"Immediately Jesus stretched out His hand and took hold of him, and said to him, 'You of little faith, why did you doubt?' When they got into the boat, the wind stopped. And those who were in the boat worshiped Him, saying, 'You are certainly God's Son!'" (Matt 14:31-33 NASB).* The storm produced faith, worship, and clarity of who Jesus is and always has been. It also showed who the disciples were and what they believed about Jesus, but the boat housed purpose and that was to get them to the other side. It took the boat to carry their faith. In that boat they recognized the power of Jesus. Sometimes we are in our situation, and God nudges us to step out of what we are in. He will call us to step out and do the miraculous if we posture our heart to follow him no matter where He goes. Understand this though: No matter what, Jesus will never leave us in the boat by ourselves.

Nine years after my dad's diagnosis, his battle with cancer worsened. The hospital we were going to here in our hometown told my dad that there wasn't anything else that could be done. The tumors kept coming back, and what they had to offer had already been tried. As you can imagine, we were devastated. We felt as if we had been dropped. Maybe you feel like that right now, but all it takes is a "suddenly" moment for everything to change. Be confident in you Savior; your best days are ahead of you. Remember the story of Shadrach, Meshach and Abednego? The furnace was set to seven times hotter than usual, and they were mocked, "Who is this God who is able to deliver you?" Maybe Satan has been telling you that nothing will change, and in fact it has gotten worse. That is a very real threat that can loom at any moment, but we need to be Christians that will rise up in the midst of our fiery trial or storm and say the words of these boys as they were told to worship an image or be thrown into the fire which meant certain death. Let's look at the response of these three Hebrew boys to the threats and mocking: "*Our God whom we serve is able to deliver us from the furnace of blazing fire; and He will deliver us out of your hand, O king. But even if He does not, let it be known to you, O king, that we are not going to serve your gods or worship the golden image that you have set up" (Daniel 3:17-18 NASB).*

Jesus would give us a "suddenly" moment. In this situation with my dad, our family was being taunted by the giant of cancer. Test result after test result looked like heat of the fiery furnace being turned up. My dad's cancer would progress from one tumor to two tumors to multiple tumors to his CEA levels going to an all-time high to chemo no longer working. We went from our hometown hospital weeping in hopelessness to the halls of MD Anderson sitting in front of the best doctors in the world. Yet we were scared and wondering when God would deliver him from this tyrant of sickness. How had this happened?

One day Mr. Henry Adams, a wealthy and generous business man who is also a great man of God, called my dad because he said the Lord placed it on his heart. He told my dad that he knew the best doctors in the world, and he could put my dad in the best medical hands with only one phone call. (At one time, Mr. Henry himself had needed a liver transplant or he would have died. He received that transplant at St. Luke's Hospital, and it saved Mr. Henry's life.) With my dad's permission, Mr. Henry contacted the doctors at St. Luke Hospital who had given him that liver transplant, and they in return contacted some friends at MD Anderson. He told my dad to not worry if money was a concern because Jesus had sent him to help. My dad hung up the phone, and that same day these doctors called my dad. That is unheard of in the medical community. Soon afterwards, my dad began treatment there with those doctors, and this opportunity extended my dad's life. They introduced him to a new procedure, and he experienced good results. His CEA levels (a marker of tumor development and activity) were supposed to be up to two times higher after the procedure. That was the normal. A week later his CEA levels had dropped 40%, and they dropped again at the following test. God has resources that we do not know about, and He is working even when we can't see. I said all that to say, when the fire is turned up seven times hotter, don't count God out. When the devil is crouching over our shoulders telling us God has forgotten about us, stand firm and tell him, "My God is able to deliver me, but even if he doesn't, I will not bow my knee to my circumstance." This brings glory to God.

Just watching Jesus work in a situation will cause many to say, *"Look! I see four men loosed and walking about in the midst of the fire without harm, and the appearance of the fourth is like a son of the gods!" Daniel 3:25 NASB*). Can Jesus be seen by onlookers in the midst of our trial? Our attitude in the fiery furnace should be, "Our God is able to deliver us, but if not, I will still serve the King of Kings and Lord of Lords." How we respond produces a testimony to those who are watching. The Bible says, *"In regard to these men that the fire had no effect on the bodies of these men nor was the hair of their head singed, nor were their trousers damaged, nor had the smell of fire even come upon them. Nebuchadnezzar responded and said, 'Blessed be the God of Shadrach, Meshach and Abed-nego'" (Daniel 3:27-28 NASB).* I liken this to my dad here. If you looked at him, you couldn't even smell the smoke of cancer on him. Though it was there, what people were seeing was not the cancer. Our trials produce a greater glory than we are even aware of.

Listen, the Bible also describes their descent into the fire this way, "*But these three men, Shadrach, Meshach and Abed-nego, fell into the midst of the furnace of blazing fire still tied up (Daniel 3:23 NASB)* He says that they "fell" into the fire. What's the message for us? We may be in the fire, and even worse, we have lost our footing, but there is another just as the fourth man seen in the fire. His name is Jesus Christ, our heavenly big brother. He will untie us and raise us up for all the world to see the miraculous sustaining power of God Almighty and for every demon in Hell to see that His power is alive even when we are looking impossibility in the face.

God doesn't send someone into our battle; he climbs into our boats or our furnaces.

Whether it is sicknesses, finances, disappointments, or losses, it is not purposeless. All of it is working for His Glory and our good. In the natural, we can't see it. When tragedy hits, when we lose a loved one, or when our dreams seems hopeless, don't think this is pointless. Don't lose faith in God. On the contrary, rise up from the ashes of despair and sow your pain into God's soil of purpose. You may water the soil with tears, but set your eyes on the eternal plans of God. Step out of the boat into the deep of His ways and grab His hand. Listen, God could have taken cancer from my dad's body, but there were years of miracles our family walked in and would have missed. Sometimes we are looking for the final delivery and miss the miraculous feeding in the desert, or the cloud by day and the fire by night. The final delivery may be healing on this side or death for some resulting in eternal healing there. Sow your pain and expect God to bless you even greater than the troubles you have faced in your waterless pit. Remember, the Bible says that the things we face here are not worthy to be compared with the things in heaven. I challenge you to become a prisoner of hope. The book of Zechariah says, "A*s for you also, because of the blood of My covenant with you, I have set your prisoners free from the waterless pit. Return to the stronghold, O prisoners who have the hope; This very day I am declaring that I will restore double to you" (Zechariah 9:11-12 NASB).* At this point in the journey, my dad was still taking his regimen of chemotherapy and continuing his doctor visits, but we continued to keep our eyes on Jesus as the storms still raged. His grace and our hope in Him were consistent.

Would you join me in this declaration of faith?

I declare that no matter what I am facing, no matter how the storm rages, no matter how battered my boat is, the anchor holds. No matter how hot the furnace gets, I know that my Jesus is with me; he will never leave me nor forsake me. He will guide and use me as I keep my eyes on Him and not the winds and the waves. He is my ever-present help in the time of trouble and the day of adversity. I will be used in mighty ways as I step out of my boat at His command. I am ready and willing to be used by the Master.

FIVE

The Staff Under My Arms

"Not forsaking our own assembling together, as is the habit of some, but encouraging one another; and all the more as you see the day drawing near."
(Hebrews 10:25 NASB)

In 2006 about a year after we'd been married, Shannon and I went to a family crawfish boil at her uncle's house. It would be my first time meeting this side of the family, and it would further God's plan for my life. While we were there, we talked to her aunt, and Shannon noticed a joy in her countenance. We could both tell something was different about her. Shannon asked her if she went to church, and she told Shannon that she did and that we should visit Family Life Church. Instantly I cringed and thought, "No way." We live over thirty miles from the church, and I didn't see any point in visiting because I would not drive thirty miles every Sunday to go to church; however, I eventually gave in and agreed to a visit because I could see that we desperately needed the Lord in our marriage.

The beginning of our marriage had taken some licks, so to speak, and honestly, I was burnt out with church and the trials I had been through. I was discouraged and feeling alone instead of connected to the body of Christ. I felt like my church experience was toxic to my relationship with God. I know people are human, Christian or not, but in a way I was blaming God for the experiences I had with people in the church. I would often ask God, "How can I call myself a Christian and not love your people?" This was simply where I was at that time. Church burnout is common today; however, it is not an excuse to stop going. The church body needs its members to be healthy and growing because the kingdom of darkness is healthy and growing.

On the first Sunday we went to Family Life Church, I was totally skeptical. I had come from a denominational background that did not believe in the baptism of the Holy Spirit with the evidence of speaking in tongues. Going back to my time in Israel, we had gone to a little Messianic Christian service, and this preacher gave an altar call for anyone who wanted to experience the baptism of the Holy Spirit. I went up, and I will never forget that experience as long as I live. I am not a flaky person at all; I will not respond to the anything that is fake to feed a false experience. I just wanted to clear that up so you know where I stand; I'm not that guy. I am very conservative. With that being said, I went up for the altar call and the Messianic Jewish preacher laid hands on me. I went down under the mighty power of the Holy Spirit, and I was speaking in other tongues. I have to say, Israel changed me forever.

I was very skeptical when it came to the manifestations of the Holy Spirit because of the way I was taught in a denominational church, but my experience changed that perception. Although I do not elevate my experience over the Word of God, my experience in Israel backed up what I read. I had seen many things in non-denominational churches on television that made me uncomfortable so even though I was baptized in the Holy Spirit and didn't really feel like I fit in the denomination I grew up in, I was scared of what I would be walking into if I went elsewhere.

Because of my view of non-denominational churches, Shannon was petrified of how I would respond at her aunt's church; however, on this particular Sunday, I felt the presence of God as soon as I walked in. I can't remember the worship or the sermon, but I remember the exhortation Pastor Todd gave. The church was going through a transitional moment, and I was so inspired by Pastor Todd's leadership in the matter. I could instantly tell that I was in a safe environment. As we left the church that Sunday, we sat in the car in silence. I could tell Shannon was troubled by what I would say, so finally she spoke up and asked me, "So what did you think?" I told her I liked it, and we could go back. Bro. Francis Martin, who is the founding pastor of Family Life Church, once told me that God told him that Family Life was going to be a hospital for the hurting. I have to say I truly believe that was definitely a word from God. I think when people who have been hurt come into the church, they come in as wounded patients, and they should find healing. However, over time they should move into a nursing or even a doctor role to other hurting patients coming in. When we came in, I was bloodied in the spirit. I told Shannon that we could go, but I wanted to slip in the back and leave right afterwards. I was not interested in getting to know anyone, especially a pastor. This is where I was, but it would not be long before that would change.

People in the church reached out to me, and it really was great to connect. A man named Steve Himel was the first person to connect with me. I remember he asked me what I wanted God to do in my life, and I told him that I wanted God to give me compassion for people. I knew that was what I needed; I needed to learn how to love people. Steve genuinely took interest in me and God used that man to help heal me. I also met some of my other closest friends here. I also met Pastor Todd who has also been a tremendous blessing. In a larger church, you don't always get to meet with the senior pastor, but he always made his way over to Shannon and me. Tonya, Pastor Todd's wife, and Felicia, Steve's wife, also became great friends to us. God is willing to use people to aid in our healing if we will just surround ourselves with people in the local church. God is in the healing business, friend. He will offer it in any area at any time, and the local church is one thing the Lord uses. God has established His church as a lighthouse for our communities.

Sunday after Sunday and Wednesday after Wednesday, people come in and out of the doors of churches and never connect. Many people in church are facing situations in life, and they feel alone all the while sitting next to someone who recently won victory over what they are facing now. Right now is the Church of the living God's best time to reach out to the hurting. Inside church buildings are lifelong connections ready to be formed. Future husbands and wives will meet there. Destinies will be changed by the people we meet in the pew. I have brothers and sisters in church who will go to battle for me without a thought, and I for them. All of this starts with connection. It begins with people reaching out to us but also us reaching out to them. It begins by laying all our pre-conceived notions and past hurts down and letting God heal and connect us with who He wants in our lives.

Destiny connects us and strengthens us. Our destiny is to be transformed into the image of Christ, to be more like him every day. God uses wisdom and counsel from people to do that. Satan knows this and that is why he doesn't want us to connect. He wants to bind us up in isolation and frustration. Satan's strategy is divide and conquer; God's strategy is connect and empower. Satan knows that there is power in unity, and that is why he is trying to fill our schedules and stack up our offenses.

I believe that you will be used by God to speak into the lives of people you connect with in your church. Some of you need healing and will possibly receive it from someone sitting next to you or someone in your small group. Some of the best counseling you will receive will be from the ones who came through what you are going through right now. Many of you need answers to issues in life, and your experience will help people in theirs. God brought you through it to help bring someone else through it. The world, as well as many in the church, is hurting, and we have the answer. That answer is Christ. Coming together in His power and authority is where we accomplish the work of the ministry, but we ourselves need to connect in the most powerful institution on planet Earth and that is the Church of Jesus Christ which is not the building, but you who are sitting in the building. I believe some of the greatest miracles we will see in the future will be in small groups within the church. I'll tell you why. When God begins to pour out His miraculous power, He won't wait until a Sunday or a Wednesday service.

I want to leave you with two verses of Scripture. The first one is in Acts- *"All the believers devoted themselves to the apostles' teaching, and to fellowship, and to sharing in meals (including the Lord's Supper), and to prayer. A deep sense of awe came over them all, and the apostles performed many miraculous signs and wonders" (Acts 2:42-43 NLT).* Then there are these verses in Psalms- *"Behold, how good and how pleasant it is For brothers to dwell together in unity! For there the Lord commanded the blessing — life forever" (Psalms 133:1,3 NASB).*

Let me pray this over you, my friend.

Heavenly Father, I come to You in the name of Your son Jesus, and I ask that You would connect Your people to a local church if they are not now presently attending one. I ask that You would help them lay down any hindrances or hurts they may have experienced. I pray, like Bro. Francis, that they find the church to be a hospital for them. I pray that if my friend is already attending a church that You would connect them with people who will speak life and help them along in the plan and purpose You have for them. Lord, would You also use my friend to be a healing agent in their local church? Amen.

SIX

Miscarriage for a New Generation

Trust in the Lord with all your heart, and do not lean on your own understanding. In all your ways acknowledge him, and he will make straight your paths.
(Proverbs 3:5-6 ESV)

I mentioned earlier about a conversation I had with Shannon at my dining room table when I wanted to hear her opinion about having children together. I had some bad relationships when I was younger, and I learned what it is like to be in an unfaithful relationship. Having experienced heartbreak after heartbreak, I had developed a mentality of distrust in relationships. During this time while my desire to have a child remained strong, I had always wanted a child but not a wife. I know that isn't a healthy thought or relationship for the child, but that is where I was in regards to relationships before Shannon. However, Shannon has truly been a blessing at truly changing my mentality in relationships. She has taught me how to trust again. During our discussion, we had determined to wait at least a year to even start trying. Since our marriage, Shannon and I had bought a house two houses down from where I grew up. I used to play in this corner lot when I was growing up so when the house was built, I was furious. As a child, I would catch the bus at the store on the corner and cut through the field to come home. I was devastated as a child having to take about twenty extra steps walking on the road instead of crossing a field so I would still cross under my neighbor's front porch and eventually he planted a bush there. The bush is actually still there today, and I now take care of it- I am even quite fond of it. It keeps people from cutting through my porch. Some people can be so nervy!

It was in this house that I feel our marriage began to thrive. I saw Dylan riding his bike through the same neighborhood I had ridden through. I coached Dylan in the same park I was coached in by my dad. Life was coming full circle. When I sit on the floor in my bedroom, I am right where I was grew up playing. Anybody who knows me knows this means a lot because I am very nostalgic- so nostalgic that I have a collection of old TV series and cartoons that I grew up watching. My intention was to be able to have my children watch everything I grew up watching. I tried it on Dylan, but he wasn't as enthusiastic as I was! He only sat through it because he knew it made me happy.

After a couple of years had passed, Shannon and I had the conversation about having children, and she said that she had changed her mind. She had not deceived me; she had simply changed her mind as people do. Honestly, it was very difficult to swallow the thought of never trying to have children. It was really hard to accept this, but I did. About a year after Shannon had decided that she didn't want to have any more children, I was sitting in my chair, and she came in with a present. Her face was glowing. I just thought it was a usual gift; I was not expecting it to be a bag with a dream in it. Shannon is a gift giver so I wasn't expecting something out of the ordinary; she is always buying me little gifts without a reason which is such a blessing. I took the bag and opened it, and there was my dream. Inside there was a pregnancy test and a little onesie. I looked up through tear-filled eyes only to see my bride fighting back tears of her own. I was taken aback because I wasn't sure what was behind her tears, but as I jumped up to hug her, I learned that they were tears of excitement and joy. I assured her that this time she would not be alone in her pregnancy, and I would be there every step of the way. I had made up my mind that she would never want for anything during this process. I can't put into words what it felt like for me. I was simply overcome with the thought of having this dream come true. I have a father's heart, and I have always felt that. We told Dylan, and he was also excited to have a brother or sister. He would have been the greatest big brother; he is so natural with kids. He will one day make an awesome father. After we told Dylan, we went two houses down to tell my mom and dad, and as you can imagine, I was so excited to tell them. It was awesome to be able to bring them such good news after the cancer diagnosis.

We arrived at their house and told them that we had a surprise for them. They were going to be biological grandparents, and as you can imagine, they were overwhelmed with joy. As we sat at the table, I saw my dad's mind wandering as he stared off into space. I know he was thinking, "What if cancer stops me from watching this child grow up?" It was a bitter-sweet moment for me, but I saw it as more fuel for him to fight. I knew the excitement and expectation would grow every single day, and while I waited, I pictured my little baby girl or boy running around the house. I saw him or her asking me for a snack and me rushing to get it just to watch them get excited. I put on those old cartoons just to imagine the joy that would come to their face as we would cuddle and make memories. I saw myself sitting in my chair with our little one, and I planned to rub his or her little head until he or she fell asleep in my daydreams. Sometimes I laid in bed and imagined what it would be like to be wakened by a little hand on mine to console him or her from a nightmare or a noise. Through it all, I laid my hands on Shannon and prayed for the development to be healthy and smooth.

As the day came for our first doctor visit, I was sleepless the night before. As I lay next to my wife, I felt my heart enlarging with love for this baby in her womb. I was also grateful that Shannon was excited and that our marriage was also growing. I thanked God for the opportunity to raise a family on a daily basis. The morning of the appointment, I woke up with a spring in my step. I went to work and did my job waiting for the doctor's appointment to come. Shannon and I met at the doctor's office, and I couldn't contain my excitement as I was trembling. I brought my phone and another camera because I wanted to cherish this memory forever. I was going to watch the video every day and share it everywhere with everyone. When we walked into the room, the nurse asked us the name, and we said, "Kaleb." We were not sure if the child was a boy or girl, but we had only thought of a boy name for now. The lights were turned off, and I readied both cameras. My hands were shaking, and I began to sweat. My heart was racing with joy. I had never before heard a baby's heartbeat during an ultrasound. As the nurse rubbed the wand on Shannon's stomach, I could see this beautiful baby, but something was wrong. I could see coloring outside the sack that housed the baby and heard nothing. I could see the tension rising in the nurse and Shannon's face. I finally heard the words, "I'm sorry, but there is no heartbeat." The nurse spent time measuring the size of the baby to determine when he or she had died. She determined that the baby had died about a week earlier. In my mind, all I kept hearing were the words that said our child was dead. My hands grew clammy, and I could only hear my heart beating in my ears. It reminded me of when the doctor had told us that my dad had cancer. I thought, "How could this happen?" I had prayed over this baby every day. I had memories and traditions already planned out. I had already decided on which cartoons I would start the baby loving. I had pictured the baby dedication at church in which I would have held up the baby like Rafiki did on *The Lion King*. At that moment, I had decided that I would pray for the baby to be raised from the dead in her womb. Since Jesus had raised a dead man from the grave who had been dead for four days, surely this would be a piece of cake. Yet, when the nurse turned off the machine and the screen went black, it felt as the window to my dream had been slammed shut.

We were all devastated, but I truly felt a wider range of emotions. I felt guilty because I had put Shannon through this. She was already going through a lot, and I was so proud of her and grateful that she had wanted to take this journey of pregnancy with me. Now she was going to have to experience a devastating tragedy that she had never experienced before, and I felt it was my fault. I couldn't help but feel like I and my family history had caused the miscarriage. All I could think about was how could God have allowed this. I shifted to a works mentality with God. "God, I know you heard Shannon's and my conversation. I know you saw how she agreed to go forward with this desire for a baby. I know you saw how our marriage was growing and improving, and it now feels like we are moving backwards." I also reminded Him that He alone was the giver of life. The nurse encouraged us that these things happen and to keep trying, and I could see in Shannon's eyes that she was more concerned for me because she knew how much this pregnancy and baby had meant to me. It was a growing moment for us because we put each other first and really came together. Shannon is one of the strongest people I have ever met, and she is so sacrificial, always putting other people first.

Still when I made it back to my truck, I lost it. Hurt, I cried out and reminded God how I was really trying harder to improve my sanctification walk before Him. I told Him, "God I prayed so hard, and I really worked hard at trying to be holy as never before." I tried to bargain in a selfish way.

Truthfully, I had done this selfishly so that all hindrances for a safe pregnancy would be halted which I know was not right, but at the time, I was trying all I knew to do. I know that we can never make Jesus indebted to us, but I was desperate. I lamented to God, and I sensed only silence. I went back to work that afternoon feeling hopeless. I felt like my world was crashing around me again, and I was thinking about Shannon and what she must be feeling. I was heartbroken, sitting in the ash of devastated dreams. Nothing looked the same as it had before that appointment. I returned to questions from my coworkers who were really there for me, and I appreciate them to this day. They knew that I was a Christian who was completely committed to Christ. I had to stay strong and maintain my witness even while inside I was so angry at God. All I could ask was "Why God?" The irony of knowing the awesomeness and power of God is that we can easily get angry with Him when we suffer trials because we know without a doubt that He can do anything. Sometimes His plans are different than ours and that can be difficult to accept. I continued to struggle as I asked Him, "How could you allow this?" So many people don't want children, and they give healthy births to many children. The afternoon dragged on, and it felt as if time lingered as the pain increased.

I still needed to tell my parents, and I knew they would grieve for Shannon and me, as well as grieve all over again for their lost babies, reliving their pain through ours. We also needed to tell Dylan and Shannon's parents. Again, the waves of guilt washed over me as I felt this was my fault for causing so many people pain. Satan will always piggyback on our grief with lies. This was the lie I kept hearing and telling myself. That night was a quiet night for Shannon and me. I remember just staring at her stomach and praying for the resurrecting power of God to invade her womb. I lay in bed that night, and all I could think was that inside of my wife's body death was present as an invader. The night before I had laid down trembling with excitement only to lay down this night paralyzed with heartache and pain. It would not be long before Shannon would officially miscarry Kaleb or our little sweet baby girl. Though expected, this was another layer of devastation. Still Shannon and I came together and made it through by the grace of God.

I know some look at miscarriage as something differently than death. I know death is a strong term to use for miscarriage, but that is exactly what it is. If you look in the book of Luke, speaking of John the Baptist the Bible says, *"For he will be great before the Lord. And he must not drink wine or strong drink, and he will be filled with the Holy Spirit, even from his mother's womb" (Luke 1:15 ESV).* The Holy Spirit does not fill anything but human beings. The Bible also says, *"And when Elizabeth heard the greeting of Mary, the baby leaped in her womb" (Luke 1:41 ESV).* We call them fetuses, but God Almighty considers babies in the womb human beings. When Rebekah was pregnant with the twins Jacob and Esau the Bible says, "*The children struggled together within her, and she said, 'If it is thus, why is this happening to me?' So she went to inquire of the Lord. And the Lord said to her, 'Two nations are in your womb, and two peoples from within you shall be divided; the one shall be stronger than the other, the older shall serve the younger'"* *(Genesis 25:22-23 ESV)*. God called them children, He had their destinies planned. In fact through foreknowledge, He plans our purposes before we are created in the womb. The great book of Jeremiah says, *"Before I formed you in the womb I knew you, and before you were born I consecrated you; I appointed you a prophet to the nations"* *(Jeremiah 1:5 ESV)*. Miscarriage is the death of a child.

Shannon and I would eventually go on to try again. The second time was planned, and once again excitement and fear greeted us at the conception. We had limped through the death of our first child, and we were not quick to tell many people because we were scared of another miscarriage. We really did not want to have to keep going back and explaining our misfortune; this was such a painful thing – to have to live it and then tell of it. I remember I kicked back into a works mentality of watching my every thought and every action. I also prayed throughout the day, and I laid hands in prayer on Shannon often. These are all good things to do in and of themselves, but I was doing it in a wrong spirit which was setting me up for a major downfall. Some kind of a way I had taken on this cloak of self-condemnation. I felt as if my performance in some strange way was shouldering the responsibility of whether our children would live or die. Then I also began to look at all the other people around us who were pregnant and I saw that none of them were dealing with any thoughts like this. While I was trying to be a good Christian, there were many people who are atheists and people of different beliefs having children, as well as many situations resulting in the births of beautiful children.

God used these moments and realizations to straighten out my theology. I cannot earn any great or good thing in my life; nor is any trial or trouble a result of failing to meet all of these godly expectations I have put on my life. Then in addition, to all of these thoughts, all of the doctor's recommendations for a healthy pregnancy also filled my mind. I remember that Shannon wouldn't even drink caffeine because we had heard that these things can result in miscarriage.

The day came for our first ultrasound for our second child. I had been fasting and praying all week for this baby to be alive and healthy. We went into the room with the nurse, and once again I had my phone and another camera with me. Our hearts were racing again as she moved that wand over Shannon's stomach. There was silence again as I now knew what to look for. I was looking to make sure there was no coloring outside the sack; I was also listening intently for the heartbeat. I can remember praying so hard during that moment, but once again to no avail. Our child was dead once again. This would go on to happen many more times. Eventually, the cute little reveals stopped. Shannon's gift bags stopped. She now began to wait to tell me until it was almost time for the first doctor's visit. The doctor would put her on progesterone and schedule the doctor's visits earlier rather than later to monitor her more closely. Meanwhile, I went through long bouts of spiritual rollercoasters where I battled in my faith. I began thinking that people would think I had a generational curse or was full of sin. In these times I prayed for hours and walked the proverbial chalk line. I fasted and prayed. I worshipped my face off. I took captive every thought. I quoted Scriptures. I declared to God, *"Your Word says no good thing will I withhold from you" (Psalm 84:11 paraphr.).* I quoted, *"Be fruitful and multiply" (Genesis 1:28 paraphr.),* and *"Ask and you shall receive, knock and it shall be opened" (Matthew 7:7 paraphr.).* I begged God, "You did it for Hannah; please do it again." I recited the prayer of Hannah and turned it into a formula. I quoted Scripture after Scripture. I prayed in faith, as well as begged and plead with God while tears rolled down my cheeks. Every time we went for the heartbeat ultrasound, I would repent and repent just in case I was unpleasing to the Lord.

As pregnancies came and went, I went through some without praying as much or laying on of hands as much. The chalk line didn't seem so clear, and yet to no avail. I began to realize that the outcome of the pregnancies had nothing to do with my performance. I prayed and prayed, but there wasn't a baby. I didn't pray as much, and there still wasn't a baby. It has to be that way; no one would have a baby or get blessed if it was based on performance. Still, it was now painful to entertain thoughts of watching those cartoons with my baby boy or girl. I stopped bringing cameras to each doctor's appointment. Each time we would sit in the ultrasound room and hear the "I'm sorry," the words made us numb as we shook our heads in unbelief. Tears no longer flowed as anger and numbness became the go-to emotion. I could hear the cement around my heart hardening towards God. As I sat in that room after the ultrasounds waiting to meet with the doctor, I looked at my wife as tears would fill her eyes. I saw her fighting them back for my sake, and my heart filled with even more love for her.

I saw the discouragement, and the great sacrifice she kept on making because she knew how badly I wanted a child. Early in our marriage I wondered if she really loved me because she was not the most physically affectionate person and that is how I received love. In that moment, the Lord let me see Shannon through His eyes, and the Lord spoke to my heart so clearly and said, "Don't you ever doubt the love of My daughter for you again." It was an "aha" moment. I saw her dealing with emotions I could not fathom nor help to ease. Our children were a part of her, and she ultimately had to process their death physically, as well as mentally and emotionally. I knew that I could never put her through this again. I hugged her with all the emotion I had left and said, "I am so sorry I keep putting you through this. We don't have to try anymore. I am so sorry. I feel the pain you are feeling, and I don't want you to feel that anymore." I understood what Jesus meant about laying down our lives for our wives. That day I came to the realization that I needed to lay down my life and my dream of a child. I had to lay down my Isaac. We left that doctor's office for the last time that day with tremendous losses, but we were closer than ever.

I now had to come to terms without ever knowing what it would be like to look down in a crib filled with a heart full of joy. I would never know what it was like to listen to the sighs as my child lay asleep in a crib. The thoughts of coming home to arms raised were a distant memory. I would never do the airplane gesture to get them to eat. I went through bouts of anger towards God. I didn't want to be the guy that you looked at in sympathy while you hugged your own child and said, "I'm glad I don't have to deal with what he is dealing with." I felt that even God didn't understand because I would tell him, "Even You have a son."

I developed a pity mentality that God could only get glory out of my life if I suffered. I told God that I would never speak about this and in no way would He get glory from this if it were up to me. I was so frustrated, pouty to be exact. I was also conflicted because at the same time I didn't want to make God like an unloving and powerless god. I hid in my own private dungeon of despair because I didn't want people to lose their faith in Him. This was not a faith-filled, powerful testimony. Even though I wasn't getting what I had long desired, I still loved God and believed the gospel. I felt robbed that my lot in life was for people to see us going through disappointment after disappointment and still hanging in there as some sort of sad inspiration. To make matters worse, we sat in church hearing songs with lyrics about God answering our deepest calls and coming to our rescue. As I heard how He is mighty to save and He can move mountains, I was saying, "But you didn't, God."

During this season, there were also times of refreshing when I would feel God comforting us. I felt like a child crawling onto his daddy's lap grabbing his face with pain in my heart and tears in my eyes saying, "God, why are you letting this happen? Please make it stop." Overall, these times of pregnancy and miscarriage would draw me close to God. No matter what situations, good or bad, if they bring us to God, in joy or in pain, then there is no better place to be. I came to realize that I had made having a baby an idol, and everything hinged on that coming to pass.

You see, I learned that even in the godliest normal desire, if that becomes the ultimatum in which we serve God, becomes evil and idolatrous. We won't come out and say that we are making something an idol- I sure didn't- but we are.

Allow me to fast forward for a moment to a class I attended years later. In the class the instructor said, "Imagine Jesus walked into that room during those moments of trial. What would you tell him?" I was told to be truthful, and I will be brutally honest with you. I pictured Jesus walking in the room with eyes full of compassion for our hurt. My heart began to race at just the thought of that moment, and I was filled with such grief and disappointment that I admitted I would tell Jesus, "Thank you for coming, but if you are not going to fix this, then please leave. I don't need another spectator. I need you to save us from this." You see that I was not in a good place. I was unraveling, and nobody knew it but me. Secretly I was engulfed in a secret battle with God that I knew I couldn't win. I was being crushed under the weight of my disappointment and frustration. My faith was being dashed on the rocks of broken dreams.

Here is the very real struggle between human desires and Christian beliefs. In spite all of these thoughts that flooded my soul, I still thought of God as being merciful for never allowing us to hear the heartbeat through all of this. I think maybe it would have plagued me more. I came to the conclusion that the Lord blesses us during the weeks when our halos are not shining so brightly, and sometimes when we are doing everything as we should and our halos are blinding each other, it seems like the heavens are still brass. Still one thing remains true. I love and thank God for every second of every pregnancy, for letting me see what being a daddy felt like even if it was for a month or so. Those small moments of times were the greatest months of my life, and yet the most painful. When we are honest with God about our feelings of loss, I believe He is big enough to take it. After all the Psalms are filled with laments from David towards God, and he was labeled as a man after God's own heart.

SEVEN

A Breakthrough, Destiny of Ministry

For the Lord sees not as man sees: man looks on the outward appearance, but the Lord looks on the heart."
(1 Samuel 16:7 ESV)

Then Samuel said to Jesse, "Are all your sons here?" And he said, "There remains yet the youngest, but behold, he is keeping the sheep." And Samuel said to Jesse, "Send and get him, for we will not sit down till he comes here." And he sent and brought him in. Now he was ruddy and had beautiful eyes and was handsome. And the Lord said, "Arise, anoint him, for this is he."
(1 Samuel 16:11-12 ESV)

In the midst of all this turmoil, I was still serving in my church by teaching a Sunday School class. Somedays, I would have fifteen people; sometimes, I would have one; sometimes, there would be no one. I would teach a wall if it would listen; all the while, I was steeped in brokenness. My dad was still battling cancer, and Shannon and I had gone through the losses of our children. After six years of serving at Family Life Church, Pastor Todd asked me if I would be willing to fill in behind the pulpit by speaking at some Wednesday night services. I was absolutely honored and floored. I was still fighting battles and trying to wade through all the disappointments. I was still battling the emptiness of not having a baby, as well as my dad's cancer as it continued to come back. By this time his chemo treatments numbered near eighty, and his surgeries entailed radiation. He also had part of his liver removed, but the tumor continued to return and multiply. This opportunity to preach alongside Pastor Todd was a life ring being thrown to me. It was as if God was saying, "Kelly, I am still listening, and I have not forgotten you."

At the time, I was working at my very dear friend Steve's company as a quality and safety manager. It was a great job, and I loved it and all my co-workers. These were the same people who had encouraged me throughout the miscarriages. I can remember one time in the midst of what I believe was the fourth miscarriage, we had a prayer meeting at the office. It was one of the most powerful times of being in God's presence that I can remember. We gathered right before it was time to go to the now dreaded ultrasound. We cried, cheered, and beat on the door of heaven for a couple of hours. We prayed the fire down, and I just knew this time was going to be different. I was full of faith by the time I left to go to that doctor's visit, and while I would love to tell you that I heard a heartbeat, we did not. I was discouraged with no children of my own, and my family was also living from test result to test result with my dad. We were always going from scan to scan as we watched his CEA blood count level (marker for possible tumor activity) going up and down. It was an emotional roller coaster.

One Sunday during this time, I was invited by Pastor Todd for an after church visit in their home. Shannon and I were good friends with Pastor Todd and his wife so we thought this was just another one of our many visits. Pastor Todd is so much more than my pastor; he is one of my best friends. He was also there for Shannon and me through all of those miscarriages. When I would call him broken and discouraged, he would weep with me. We are so lucky to have him in our lives. We visited with them in their living room that afternoon, and that day my life would change forever. He asked me if I would come on staff as an associate pastor. I can remember hearing those words, and my spirit leaped for joy inside of me. Shannon knew it was my heart's desire. Pastor Todd told me that while he had seen me faithfully serving around the church and tending the sheep, so to speak, it was the Lord who had chosen me. He assured me that God had chosen me just as he chose David. David was a man after God's own heart the Bible says, even though he didn't always act like it. God saw beyond my hurt and frustration. Take courage. God sees the heart even when it is battered and bruised. He blesses who we are and where we are. He knows who we will become and where we are going. We are all a work in progress and no one has arrived. I was being faithful in the small things, and the Lord rewarded me with another shot at my dream.

Ministry was a real eye opener for me; it was a real training ground. It was a time when the Lord would stretch me and really help me to gain some perspective in all the things I was going through. After a couple of weeks of being on staff, I was called out to a hospital visit where a dear family was in the middle of having to make a tough medical decision. The last time, I was a part of such a tragedy was when we had received the devastating news about my dad. Remember, I told you I had been unable to comfort my parents because I was paralyzed with grief and fear. I came in as a rookie pastor right into the most devastating time in this family's life, and they were looking to me for guidance and assurance that everything was going to be ok. The husband lay there as I was met by his family in the hallway. I was trembling, not wanting to do or say the wrong thing. They told me that they were faced with the decision of whether or not they should take him off of life support, and they didn't know what to do. Honestly, I did not know what to do or say. My heart broke and ached for them since my own difficult experiences fueled my compassion for this family. Compassion is one thing I had struggled with and prayed for. Little did I know that my trials and difficult times were unlocking compassion. These experiences allowed me to empathize with people in difficult circumstances and out of that grew genuine compassion. Compassion grew as I prayed with them, and as I was finishing, I saw Bro. Francis, our founding pastor, walking down the hallway. The moment looked like it was shot in slow motion with white doves following him down the hallway. (That was a joke; there weren't really any doves.) I thought, "Thank you, Jesus, for sending him my way!" He flawlessly took control of the situation. He knew what to say and exactly how to say it. I was watching a giant in the faith comfort, console, and lead. I will never forget how just his presence caused the family to draw strength and confidence. This was a moment of growth for me because I had always been the guy who had removed myself from circumstances similar to this so as to not say or do the wrong thing. I was the silent guy who sent a text message and prayed in the background. God was showing me that I needed to break out of that because one day I would need to be the person offering comfort.

God brought me back to that day with my dad and showed me that Jesus had been there to comfort us; we just hadn't seen it at that time. With the comfort He offered, we could have comforted each other. As Paul said, "*Blessed be the God and Father of our Lord Jesus Christ, the Father of mercies and God of all comfort, who comforts us in all our affliction so that we will be able to comfort those who are in any affliction with the comfort with which we ourselves are comforted by God" (2 Cor 1:3-4 NASB).* It would be during my ministry experience that God would begin to reveal truths to me as I prepared my messages. It seemed as if every message given to me by the Lord was geared towards things like suffering, how to deal with it, and what perspective to take while enduring suffering. Through the development of those messages, God would speak and reveal levels of healing. It would be healing that would be vital in the days to come.

EIGHT

Have You Considered My Servant________?

The LORD said to Satan, "Have you considered My servant Job? For there is no one like him on the earth, a blameless and upright man, fearing God and turning away from evil."
(Job 1:8 NASB)

I have a question I'd like to ask you, and it is a question that I had to answer for myself. The question is, "Can God trust me with His glory during a trial?" When bad things come upon people, sometimes, they will tend to curse God. Some say it is lack of faith, but I have to wonder. You see, when we have such faith in God who is all powerful and who we know can stop anything, frustration often comes from knowing that God is more than able to deliver us. That frustration does not come from a lack of faith in God; it comes from a battle of the wills. The battle is our will versus God's will which digs even deeper into what we believe about God. One question we ask is "Why does God allow this?" Another question is "Why doesn't God stop this?" It is not a question of if He can; the real question is "What is He doing in this?" Let's turn our attention to one of the greatest men of God in one of the greatest books of the Bible. It is a book that bears his name- the book of Job. Job is the oldest book in the Bible, and this book peels back the veil on so many issues in our own lives. This book addresses the weighty issues of life; every chapter is full of life application. If you are enduring long-lasting trials, this is the book to read.

The book of Job changes the way we view suffering by helping us to understand the purpose of suffering and why it happens. The suffering of Job was initiated by God. God removed the hedge of protection and gave Satan access to Job's life. Job is a prime example of a question I always hear, "Why do bad things happen to good people?" I have two responses to this. First, no one is good; as Jesus says in Luke, *"Why do you call me good? No one is good except God alone" (Luke 18:19 ESV).* The Bible calls us just or unjust, which means saved or lost, righteous or unrighteous. These are the only two positions in the kingdom of God. Our righteousness and goodness only come from Christ. Secondly the Bible adds, *"He causes His sun to rise on the evil and the good, and sends rain on the righteous and the unrighteous" (Matt 5:45 NASB).* Christians often believe that because they are Christians and live holy lives, they should not have to deal with troubles. They believe that troubles should be experienced by non-Christians living unholy lives. If you feel this way, then it is evident that you have not understood the battle before you. The problem with this belief is that it is manipulation, and by that I mean it is a belief that causes us to believe God is indebted to us. One needs to look no further than Job to see that bad things sometimes happen to godly people because they are godly.

When we consider Job, we have to conclude that he was a righteous man because God said he was. The story begins - *"There was a man in the land of Uz, whose name was Job, and that man was blameless, upright, fearing God, and turning away from evil" (Job 1:1 NASB).* God called Job righteous, which leads us to a truth- the righteous are not exempt from suffering. Many people today think that living rightly exempts us from attacks. To live righteously is not a safe zone; it is a product of salvation. The Bible also calls Job blameless, not sinless, meaning he was beyond reproach in who he was and his lifestyle and had a holy fear of God. In addition, he was a blessed man. God's blessing was all over him as the Bible recounts his blessings- *"And seven sons and three daughters were born to him. His possessions also were 7,000 sheep, 3,000 camels, 500 yoke of oxen, 500 female donkeys, and very many servants; and that man was the greatest of all the men of the east. And his sons used to go and hold a feast in the house of each one on his day, and they would send and invite their three sisters to eat and drink with them. And it came about, when the days of feasting had completed their cycle, that Job would send and consecrate them, rising up early in the morning and offering burnt offerings according to the number of them all; for Job said, "Perhaps my sons have sinned and cursed God in their hearts." Thus Job did continually" (Job 1:2-5 NASB).* These verses tell us that Job had a close knit family who gathered together for their birthdays. His children desired to be around him; he was a family man. All of his material needs were met; he was a successful businessman. He had sheep for clothing and food, camels for transportation, oxen to plow for food, and a large employee base. Job was also a prayer warrior; he offered sacrifices for his kids in case they had sinned. He was the king and priest of his house. Now let me ask you this, do you bat in his league? He was the least likely person to suffer based on his right standing with God. Here is what you need to understand, his trial came upon him not as discipline or because he was sinning; on the contrary, it came upon him because he was blameless. God singled him out because he was worthy to be an example. That's a different level of Christianity right there. This flies in the face of what we want to believe. It is a matter of perspective. The Bible says, "*that I may know Him and the power of His resurrection and the fellowship of His sufferings, being conformed to His death*" *(Philippians 3:10 NASB)*. We grow in grace when we suffer.

Now let's look at his trial- "*Now there was a day when the sons of God came to present themselves before the Lord, and Satan also came among them. The Lord said to Satan, 'From where do you come?' Then Satan answered the Lord and said, 'From roaming about on the earth and walking around on it.' The Lord said to Satan, 'Have you considered My servant Job? For there is no one like him on the earth, a blameless and upright man, fearing God and turning away from evil.' Then Satan answered the Lord, 'Does Job fear God for nothing? Have You not made a hedge about him and his house and all that he has, on every side? You have blessed the work of his hands, and his possessions have increased in the land. But put forth Your hand now and touch all that he has; he will surely curse You to Your face.' Then the Lord said to Satan, 'Behold, all that he has is in your power, only do not put forth your hand on him.' So Satan departed from the presence of the Lord" (Job 1:6-12 NASB).* Before you draw conclusions about this story, context is the key. I believe with all my heart that the level God will use us is the level to which we will be challenged. Satan will always target the influential for Christ because in his selecting he is looking to destroy those who are being influenced by that individual. If we are a father or a mother, Satan will seek to destroy us to try to destroy our children. Our marriages are under attack like never before, and we can see the unraveling of our society before our very eyes. We are producing a parentless generation that Hollywood is more than happy to raise.

One thing about spiritual warfare is that the closer we are to the front lines, the heavier the fire power raining down on us will be. The farther we go in our walk, the greater the resistance we will face. If we look at modern warfare tactics, even now we will notice it. If we take for instance, the fight on terrorism, they are always hunting down the ones in authority because it destroys and thwarts the plan of those that are taking the orders. It is no secret that those who desire to live godly will suffer persecution. The Bible says, "*Indeed, all who desire to live godly in Christ Jesus will be persecuted" (2 Tim 3:12 NASB).* It also says, "*Beloved, do not be surprised at the fiery ordeal among you, which comes upon you for your testing, as though some strange thing were happening to you; but to the degree that you share the sufferings of Christ, keep on rejoicing, so that also at the revelation of His glory you may rejoice with exultation. If you are reviled for the name of Christ, you are blessed, because the Spirit of glory and of God rests on you" (1 Peter 4:12-14 NASB).* So when we are in battle think of the sufferings of those who have come before us; the biblical patriarchs and finally Jesus, the greatest of all, suffered. We should know we are in good company. Jesus was the most loving, compassionate human being who ever lived, and He was crucified by the very people whom He came to bring life. Jesus said, *"In this world you shall have tribulation" (John 16:33 paraphr.).* I said all of this to tell you that we go through things, whether it is self-inflicted, Satan and his cohorts, or allowed by God. Tribulation happens.

The second truth, I want to bring out is that we need to keep a heavenly perspective in the midst of suffering. There may be a heavenly purpose we do not see. Allow me to explain. The Bible says, *"Now there was a day when the sons of God came to present themselves before the Lord, and Satan also came among them" (Job 1:6 NASB).* This is an ordinary day. This was a Monday or Tuesday or any day of the week. On this particular day, the angels who are sent out to carry out God's work reported back to give an account. The sovereignty and authority of God demands that everyone- even the angels- give an account. God is supreme over everything, and everyone is accountable to Him. No matter what a person believes, whether they are atheist, agnostic, or whatever is believed, they are still accountable to God. Picture this scene in your mind: along with the angels along comes the devil. He is the devil, but he is God's devil. In other words, God has Satan on a leash, and he can never step outside of what God allows. Satan is our real adversary. He is mentioned throughout the entire Bible from Genesis to Revelation.

I want to look beyond the stars into the third heaven and hear the conversation between God and Satan. The Bible says, *"And the Lord said to Satan, 'From where do you come?' Then Satan answered the Lord and said, 'From roaming about on the earth and walking around on it'" (Job 1:7 NASB).* God knew the answer; he was making Satan give an account. Satan was doing what he does- roaming the Earth seeking someone to devour. Then the conversation turns, and God aks, *"Have you considered My servant Job? For there is no one like him on the earth, a blameless and upright man, fearing God and turning away from evil"(Job 1:8 NASB).* Now catch this, God initiated the challenge. He also selected him because he was righteous. Here is the hope in this- God already knew Job would prevail. Allow me to ask you a question. Is our life worthy of a test? Are our lives worthy of God saying, "Watch this guy or lady right here."? Consider also the story of Stephen who was stoned for his faith. As Stephen was being stoned to death for his faith, the Bible says that Jesus stood up from His throne as He looked at Stephen's face glowing from the glory of God. Are our lives worthy of pulling Jesus to His feet like He did with Stephen? Stephen's greatest threat and trial produced one of the greatest men of God to ever live, Paul the Apostle. He was there holding the coats of those stoning him and seeing Stephen glorify Jesus in the midst of the circumstance that was killing him produced an experience that would change Paul's destiny. Ultimately, it would change our destinies as well. How many times have we read the very words of Paul that were inspired by the Holy Spirit which produced life-giving hope in the midst of our trials?

You and I do not know who is watching as we encounter our suffering and trials, but we must believe that it is producing a greater weight and glory. Listen to this verse Paul wrote: "*For this light momentary affliction is preparing for us an eternal weight of glory beyond all comparison, as we look not to the things that are seen but to the things that are unseen. For the things that are seen are transient, but the things that are unseen are eternal" (2 Cor 4:17-18 ESV).* I look at my situation with the miscarriages and think, what was Satan trying to stop? He didn't stop me, and the devil still has to deal with me and my purpose which is to destroy his sandcastle kingdom. My fuel is now to pray for people who deal with life-changing trials and the wood that fuels my fire are my disappointments. Ponder this question: Instead of asking, "Why me, God?" ask, "What does God know about my future, and what is God trying to show Satan through my trials?" I look at God like a proud father who says, "Let my son play in the game, and watch him dominate." I think of Dylan when I coached him in basketball. He was one of my best players, and I would put him against any player in a one-on-one situation. Did I think he would win every battle? No. There were a lot of guys out there with different skill sets, but I had enough confidence in the skill and drive that were in him. I knew that what was in him would produce his best every time he got the ball. That is all I expected from him. I think the same is true with God. He knows what is in us, and He knows what our purpose is. Some will be assigned different levels of battles which will produce a greater anointing for a greater reason. He just wants us to see beyond our prayer list and move forward to influence His kingdom. He is producing a skill set of perseverance and a greater glory for His name in our life. That skill set of perseverance is produced in the fire of battle and will inspire others in their trials. Notice something else about the verse we just read. It says that whatever we are facing is momentary and light. That may seem insulting to some who are in the fight of their lives, but it really is true. In comparison of eternity and the glory of God and heaven, every trouble is microscopic in comparison.

Have you ever thought that things may come upon you because you are doing everything right? Remember also the question I asked earlier, "Can God trust you with tragedy? Or will you curse him and throw Him to the side when it gets bad? Do you think God thinks highly enough of you to say to Satan, 'Have you considered my servant____________?" This is having a heavenly perspective. Notice the military- it hands out medals of the highest honors to the soldiers who persevere in the battles that the commanders put them in. Paul should be considered a five star general in the Army of God. For example, in Philippians he states, "*For to you it has been granted for Christ's sake, not only to believe in Him, but also to suffer for His sake, experiencing the same conflict which you saw in me, and now hear to be in me" (Philippians 1:29-30 NASB).* Paul's conflict existed because he was a mighty man of God who was making headway in God's kingdom, and his suffering and perseverance inspire us all. His suffering came from Satan using people, but it produced the glory of God in Paul's life. In Acts, God tells Ananias to seek out Saul (later to become Paul), the persecutor of the Christians, when Ananias is hesitant, God says, *"Go, for he is a chosen instrument of Mine, to bear My name before the Gentiles and kings and the sons of Israel;* ***for I will show him how much he must suffer for My name's sake."*** *(Acts 9:15-16 NASB).* Peter would tell us, *"But even if you should suffer for the sake of righteousness, you are blessed"(1 Peter 3:14 NASB).* The word "blessed" means we are highly favored. Suffering should not produce a lament that says, "Woe is me." Instead, it should make all of heaven say, "Wow! Look at his perseverance in the fire." Suffering to the disciples was a badge of honor because they knew it was furthering the kingdom of God.

Job did not know what was at stake here, but Satan attacked God verbally, as well as questioned Job's integrity towards God with one sentence: *"Then Satan answered the Lord, 'Does Job fear God for nothing?'" (Job 1:9 NASB).* I asked this question earlier, "Can God trust you with His Glory?" Here is what I mean- Satan made it sound like Job only served God because God has blessed him. In essence, he told God that He had to bless people to get worshipped. He believed that God needed to do things for people to get them to love you Him; he taunted that God was not worthy of being loved just because He is God. In his opinion, Job only loved God because He had blessed Job. How many times have I heard people say, "Well if this is serving God, I don't know if I can."? You may have even said that at one time. I had to answer this question in my own life, and I want you to think about it. If God never answered another prayer, if you never had another goose bump and the heavens became brass is God worth pushing through for? This is the most beautiful picture of suffering for the glory of God. I am going to make a bold statement, but I believe it to be true. You will never be able to answer this until you come through a desert season or a major trial. Let me tell you, God loves you because He loves you. The question is "Do you love God because He is God?"

Some may not feel like they are protected or defended, but look at the observation Satan makes. *"Have You not made a hedge about him and his house and all that he has, on every side? You have blessed the work of his hands, and his possessions have increased in the land" (Job 1:10 NASB).* Satan acknowledged the hedge; maybe he had been trying to attack him all this time. Being the most righteous man on all the earth surely grabbed Satan's attention before this day. It is hard to not wonder if this type of statement was made of me: *"But put forth Your hand now and touch all that he has; he will surely curse You to Your face" (Job 1:11 NASB).* Maybe it sounded like this, "If Kelly doesn't get his greatest desire met, he will curse you. If Kelly's dad dies, he will surely walk away from you." What does Satan's question sound like in your case? Maybe it is your health or financial ruin? Maybe it is being single for the rest of your life? We all have things that we attempt to hold God against the wall with. We silently in the depths of our souls may have this thing that could be the deal breaker. If God allows this to happen or not happen, we are willing to throw in the towel, but the true test of serving God is preserving when everything is coming against you. Will we serve God only in the good times? This is the dilemma, and this is where we lose people.

This can feel very frightening; we may feel like Satan can just have his way with us. We may also feel isolated and as if God is unconcerned about what we are facing. I want to assure you that God is in the midst. Satan cannot just do what he wants with us. God ultimately is still protecting and sovereignly watching. We see this in God's statement to Satan: "*Then the Lord said to Satan, 'Behold, all that he has is in your power, only do not put forth your hand on him.' So Satan departed from the presence of the Lord" (Job 1:12 NASB).* Satan is allowed access, but God still has parameters in which Satan is allowed to operate. God is in charge no matter what circumstances come our way. God used this situation for the glory of Himself, and it inspires billions who read this book of Job.

Before looking more deeply at Job's trial, I want to look at another aspect of keeping a heavenly perspective; we should always keep our eyes on the big picture. The big picture is the glory of God. The big picture is not what happens here on this earth, but the glory of God transcends Earth and shouts through the heavens. There is a world going on beyond the stars. This present world is only a small part of our existence. With that being said, what if an earthly trial is producing a heavenly teaching to heavenly beings? Look at this verse, "I*t is all so wonderful that even the angels are eagerly watching these things happen" (1 Peter 1:12 NLT).* In other words, angels watch our lives in awe; the church is the school for angels. The Bible also says in Hebrews that we are surrounded by a great cloud of witnesses. I believe that means that many of those that have passed on are watching from the grandstands in heaven cheering us on.

The worst day of Job's life produced the greatest teaching on how to respond on the worst day of our lives. Satan descended to the Earth to find a hedgeless yard. With great fury, he unleashed his wrath. On a normal day while the family was gathered in the midst of the oldest son's birthday party, Job's servant comes dashing through the screen door in sheer horror escaping death himself to bring the news that catastrophe had visited them; he reports, "*The oxen were plowing and the donkeys feeding beside them, and the Sabeans attacked and took them. They also slew the servants with the edge of the sword, and I alone have escaped to tell you" (Job 1:14-15 NASB).* Job had endured a terrorist attack. Instantly this terrorist band of thieves came and killed the servants and stole Job's cattle. Likewise, we see these same types of attacks and know that the powers of darkness are behind it. Today, Satan has used deception and has so filled hearts with rage and has provoked them to wreak havoc on the people of God. Make no mistake; Satan is behind all of these shootings and mass killings. He is behind the political rhetoric, just as he incited the Pharisees to scream, "Give us Barabas!" The father of lies incited the killing of John the Baptist. He used Judas and dropped him like a rag doll when he was done. Satan is the god of this world, and he is using all of these things and people to further his cause and create division on every level. He knows his time is short. Here is a fact, Satan is behind everything going on in this country and ultimately around the world, but we watch the news and blame people. Notice that the church and Israel are getting the brunt of all of this. I can assure you when the last shot is fired and the dust settles, we will be victorious because the King of Kings is coming back and of His kingdom there shall be no end!

To continue Job's story, the Bible tells us that while the first servant was giving his report to Job, "*another also came and said, 'The fire of God fell from heaven and burned up the sheep and the servants and consumed them, and I alone have escaped to tell you'"* *(Job 1:16 NASB).* Some type of lighting storm had destroyed all 7,000 sheep and servants immediately. Imagine the cataclysmic attack as fire is raging on his property. Then the Bible continues and says, "*While he was still speaking, another also came and said, 'The Chaldeans formed three bands and made a raid on the camels and took them and slew the servants with the edge of the sword, and I alone have escaped to tell you'" (Job 1:17-18 NASB).* Another messenger running for his life burst through the doors and said the Chaldeans came and stole the camels and killed the servants. The Chaldeans eventually formed the Babylonian empire that would one day take the Jewish people into bondage. This is a picture of bondages of all sorts that plague the people of God. We have seen terror, weather catastrophe, and now bondage.

Still the worst was yet to happen to Job. As he was trying to absorb these losses, "*another also came and said, 'Your sons and your daughters were eating and drinking wine in their oldest brother's house, and behold, a great wind came from across the wilderness and struck the four corners of the house, and it fell on the young people and they died, and I alone have escaped to tell you'"* *(Job 1:18-19 NASB).* A tornado-like wind came and took out the house with his ten children, killing them instantly. However, do not look only at Job's loses; I want you also notice that in the midst of catastrophe, God sends messengers. Unfortunately, they were not messengers of good news, but I believe we can bring messages of hope to those around us when trouble is breaking loose in their lives. We need to recognize that we are at war with a real devil. He and his cohorts do real harm, and as children of God we need to grow into soldiers of the Most High and arm ourselves against all the plans of the enemy. We are to put on the armor of God every day. We are to stay alert because we may not deal with devastation like this, but we know that storms will come, and we need to stay rooted and grounded in Jesus. If we do this, when they do come we will not get swept away by disappointment and fear. We can rest assured that God is sovereign over any trial we find ourselves in and know that He will work everything for His glory and our good. He is never detached, and he sees every aspect of it. Think for a moment of Job as he is standing over the graves of his ten children. I am certain that there were questions as we would also have. Can you relate to Job? Have you experienced devastation that has driven you to the ground in deep agony? I can- many times. I would imagine he was weeping in deep agony lying prostrate because the Bible says, "*Then Job arose and tore his robe and shaved his head, and he fell to the ground and worshiped" (Job 1:20 NASB).* I submit to you that this is the hard part, but it says Job arose. Job arose to a new way of life, but he had the same God. The key is he arose. He didn't stay down. I want to tell you, we have to get off the mat. We have to mourn; we have to process as Job did by tearing his robe and shaving his head. This was Job's time to grieve, but after that time, he rose. I am sure that Satan was waiting for Job to curse God. Satan was waiting for, "This is what I get for serving You? Or maybe he was waiting for, "How could You let this happen? You were supposed to help me." Maybe he even thought Job would cry out, "If You are a loving God then…? Don't You see what I am going through? Don't You care?" Satan heard none of this. Job simply worshipped. This nearly inconceivable worshipping came from knowing God deeply before God had blessed him. He had a view of God that many don't have today. I can see Job lying in ash. I can see him looking like a mad man with a shaved head and torn clothes. I can see him grasping for breath in between cries, looking through a smoke- filled sky worshipping God. I can see him weak and barely able to lift his hands but trying to see through burning tears as he musters up strength to look to Heaven. I think it is fair to say that he had a broken heart, but I am sure there was also an assurance. This to me is proof that God and man can be in real relationship. Job had no Bible, no worship band, no life group, or no podcast to get him through; all he had was a real relationship with God. It is good to have the Bible and worship music, but these things should fuel what has already been done in your heart when you came to know him. The Bible says that he did not sin or blame God (Job 1:22). In a sense, he was submitting all of this into God's hands because he had a deep abiding trust that already prepared him to handle any adversity. He didn't have to surrender all to God because in Job's mind it was already God's. It was developed in the good times, and it prepared him for this bad time. Receiving Christ is one thing, but walking it out is another thing. It is the hardest part. The way we handle devastation cuts through the clichés of Christianity. It answers the question Satan posed, "Will Job worship God for nothing?" God can say, "Yes," and there is the proof. That is a question you and I must answer, and I would challenge you to think about that before you face difficult circumstances. Put your name there. Will __________ worship God for nothing?

The last point I want to make about is Job's response. It shows the state of Job's heart which glorified God in Heaven to Heaven. After his tragic losses, *"He said, 'Naked I came from my mother's womb, and naked I shall return there. The Lord gave and the Lord has taken away. Blessed be the name of the Lord' through all this Job did not sin nor did he blame God" (Job 1:21-22 NASB).* This is a declaration of what was already known in his heart- that God is good all the time. God is sovereign. He alone gives, and He takes away. Job did not have to understand the why; he just kept his eyes on God. Even if he knew God was not causing this, he knew God was sovereign and in full control. He acknowledged that every good thing is a gift from God and that He can give it or remove it. Job knew that God had full authority over all the aspects of his life, and he trusted God knowing that. We need to remember this; even in the midst of turmoil, God has a plan, and though we may experience hurt or crushing, ultimately it is part of a bigger perfect picture that God is painting. The most beautiful and powerful songs are written in times of pain. That is the difference between having a higher view of God than ourselves. Think about the missionaries who leave their plans and go to places where they can be killed just for being a Christian. They go and live in intense danger. Do you think they do that for their own glory? Absolutely not. Many die nameless to us, but their names thunder through the heavens. They have gone, knowing they will go for His glory, and if they die, they gain. These missionaries are not being killed for goosebumps; they are being killed because of a real relationship with Jesus. I am afraid many of us are so far from that; many of us buckle under the weight of an unanswered prayer. If we believe that God's plans are all about us, then we will be crushed when troubles come our way. If we believe this, we will blame God and run away from him and to things that will destroy. Our hearts need to be postured in such a way that we only want what God wants no matter what devastation comes because we trust that God will use it for a greater good. It will be perfect because He is perfect. I want to encourage you to live your life and know that everything is about God. Keep in mind that it is about His purpose, and His glory. If we dwell on that perspective, we will persevere no matter what trial comes. I have sat in church and worshipped through burning tears in ash and worshipped when everything was going right. Can I be perfectly honest with you, friend? Those times of tears grew me more than the good times. Those tears watered the ground that helped me stand and grow today.

Job could not see the challenge in Heaven; just like we can't see the why? We go to the grave without an answer sometimes, but true worship and devotion is worshipping in the ash under the dark clouds. True faith is trusting God when He seems silent and serving in spite while continuing to live with integrity. Keep seeking God's purpose even when it is not working out. My friends, this is Christianity. Anything else is a figment of what we wish it was. Jesus said, "Follow me," and it is not optional. It is a command, and it is not for a brief time; it is now through the ash, the mud, the storm, the off road journeys, and the darkness. The end result is beyond our imagination. Job knew that all of God's ways are still perfect. He knew God was still worthy because His worth wasn't based on what he had or didn't have. This is the same decision you and I must make as we walk with God in the midst of our struggle. We can choose to bless His name or not. What do we do when these things come upon us? How do we respond? We respond like Job did- by worshiping. Worship because God is worthy. Worship because He is sovereign. Worship because He is able to work all things out for his glory. In the midst of all the attacks, Job knew that God was above all of that, and that is where he fixed his eyes.

Can we make this faith declaration together?

Lord, I bless You. I worship You. Lord, I don't understand
this, but I love You, and I always will. No matter what
may come, I will choose to believe that You have the

best in mind for me. Lord, I will choose to glorify You in every situation. I thank You that You are watching over me and protecting me. I choose to declare that You are good in every situation and circumstance. Amen!

NINE

Serving God When He Seems Silent

I am worn out waiting for your rescue, but I have put my hope in your word.
My eyes are straining to see your promises come true. When will you comfort me?
(Psalms 119:81-82 NLT)

Many compare the spiritual seasons in life with the seasons in nature. Spring brings newness of life. Summer is the season when many of us spend time with our families taking vacations and making memories. Fall is my favorite season because it launches us into the excitement of the holiday season, as well as football. The cooler weather also makes this season in South Louisiana more enjoyable. This season was always my dad and I's favorite time. When we were cutting grass, it also meant the work load slowed down. Winter then approaches, and it is a time when warmth turns to cold and things stop growing. Many people experience depression during this time. The holidays can be painful times for those who have dealt with loss. For me, it was always a reminder that I didn't have small children to wake me up on Christmas morning. However, once Dylan became a part of my life, I would rush into Dylan's room and jump on his bed to wake him up. This began a yearly challenge and tradition to see who would wake up earlier and who would get to whose bed first. In my family, my dad and I put up a Christmas village every year, and I always looked forward to that. My dad and I would stand back and admire all the people and little children we put playing in the village because miscarriage and cancer did not exist in our village.

As in nature, there are also seasons in the life of a Christian, without sounding cliché. These seasons are normal in our Christian experience. As in the winter, we sometimes have seasons of depression. During these times, we often feel as if God is silent. This is a normal feeling, and even David, a man after God's own heart, dealt with this. In the great book of Psalms, David says, *"I am weary with my crying out; my throat is parched. My eyes grow dim with waiting for my God" (Psalms 69:3 ESV).* You don't have to be a Bible scholar to see that David dealt with depression and felt helpless at times. We all face pits of depression when it seems all hope is gone, on the job or in our finances. We also feel it in relationships or in the sickness that threatens to destroy you. Divorce may rip normal life from you. It is as if everything is magnified during the winter time especially after the hype of the holidays. Depression can lead to feelings of complacency and that can be very draining. We feel like David felt when God seems to have gone silent on us. It is during these times of deep sadness that it seems like every demon in hell is breathing down our necks. During those times I would remind myself, *"He will never leave me nor forsake me" (Deut. 31:6 paraphr.).* God is God, and that does not change. To the young person whose future looked so bright but is crippled by our economy, Ephesians says, *"God is able to do above and beyond what we can think or ask" (Eph. 3:20 paraphr.).* To the high school student who is engulfed in the cares of schedules and tests, Isaiah reminds us, *"God will keep our minds in perfect peace whose mind is steadfast on Him" (Isaiah 26:3 paraphr.).* To the one whose marriage is falling apart, God is able to resurrect that love that drew you together and move in that situation and raise you up above what is killing your marriage. In every case, I say, nothing shall be impossible to us who believe. I want to tell you it is never hopeless for God has said in Jeremiah, *"I know the plans I have for you, plans to prosper you" (Jer. 29:11 paraphr.).* We need to call these things to our minds and feed our faith.

David often cried out to God writing, *"I am weary with my moaning; every night I flood my bed with tears; I drench my couch with my weeping. My eye wastes away because of grief" (Psalms 6:6-7 ESV).* Our brokenness speaks to God because Psalms also says, *"The Lord is near to the broken hearted" (Psalm 34:18 ESV).* Our tears are the language of the soul. In our darkest moments, in our pleading and waiting, push the thought far away from you that God is not listening. Let me give you an example. A while back I had a rough couple of weeks. I had the flu, and I was physically destroyed and limited to a recliner for the entire week. I could not do anything; I couldn't even read. Now before you say that is not a big deal, let me tell you that I am a compulsive reader often reading up to five books at a time. No matter what I am going through or dealing with, I am never in a place where I have no desire to read. During this time my mom and dad were at MD Anderson getting scanned to see how everything was going. Worry had come in and seized my already sick body as I began to dwell on a possible bad report. I would try to pray, but I couldn't even move my lips. I was so drained. I knew my dad would get his results at 10:00 am As 9:00 am approached, I kept trying to pray, but ultimately I couldn't. Then 10:00 am came, and I still hadn't received word. At that time, I had made up my mind that I was going to get up, and no matter what I was going to pray until the burden lifted. I began to walk around the house, and I started praying against what I was feeling. As I began to pray in the spirit, I began to feel vitality coming into my body. About 11:00 am, I finally received a text from my mom saying, "We are good." From that moment, I felt I was on the upswing of this sickness; however, it had been an extremely slow recovery, not only physically but spiritually. I had been feeling attacked like never before, and it literally felt like the flu had gotten into my soul. The takeaway is that I have to fight against what I am feeling; however, I do not want you to confuse fighting with working. Sometimes we feel like we have to do something to get out of our spiritual rut; for example, we think we have to read or do some other activity to be reconnected with God; however, oftentimes we simply need to do what the Psalmist says, *"Be still before the Lord and wait patiently for him" (Psalm 37:7 ESV).* Listen, I don't know what you have been told, but this Christian walk is a fight, and we have to fight through some things until God moves on our faith. However, there is also a beneficial balance that resting in the Lord can bring. The Bible also says, *"They that wait on the Lord shall renew their strength" (Isaiah 40:31 paraphr.).* Waiting is trusting, having a dependence on Him and not on our abilities. I found this out on my own during my battle with the flu. My strength and vitality came not because I read or did something, but because I waited on the Lord. When you are sick, Satan will piggy back on your physical condition and try to go for the jugular of your spirit. When that happens we must stand in faith, stand in joy, and stand in the strength that was provided at the cross. It is not a fight of works, but a fight of faith. Listen, God has provided everything we need, but our fight is a fight of staying and operating in the graces provided. Feelings contradict what we know by faith because faith is not a feeling. We stand in faith and our emotions line up, not the other way around. There are many days I don't feel saved or I don't feel victorious, but I still am. There are days, I don't feel like a husband or dad, but I still am. My identity is not in my feeling, but my position. Likewise, my righteousness is not in my feelings. It is in the position of righteousness Christ's death has placed me in. I am victorious not because of what my circumstances look like, but because in Christ I am seated above my circumstances. That is where we draw our strength.

Even though we may know these things, how do we apply them? First, I think we should be thankful that we belong to Jesus. When we know we belong to him, we also know that He has taken responsibility of us. He is our Lord and Savior, and that is priceless. To belong to someone who is all powerful and always looking out for us is the safest place to be. That assures me that no matter what- even if I do not have the strength to hold His hand- He is still holding mine. It reminds me of a picture my mom has. It is a picture of a man going under water and there is Jesus with His nail-pierced hands holding up the man who seemed worn out. In the second half of verse 12, Paul writes, *"Christ Jesus has made me his own" (Phillipians 3:12 ESV).* Our security is in His ability to hold us and rooted in His faithfulness not ours. When depression comes, we may feel that we need to find a verse to encourage us, but what if we have no desire to grab our Bible? We are not left alone. Our relationship with God is a two-way relationship, and when we can't reach up, he is reaching down. Just look up. I believe that it is a joy for the Lord to rescue us from our despair. As a parent, don't you like when your children need you? When we become Christians, we are justified by His death as if it were a legal transaction that took place in heaven. That legal ownership has transferred us from darkness to light, from slavery to freedom. That, my friend, is a reason to be joyful.

Let me give you an example of taking ownership. I have an English Mastiff named TeBeaux (pronounced te – bow). I love my dog. My wife and I take care of our dog, but when we are not home, he stays in a large kennel. There are days when he has to stay in there for eight hours a day, but we keep him cool by running a big fan on him. He also lives in the house in the air conditioning or heating, depending on the season. He is always fed, always has water, and is always taken out to potty. We don't do that because he asks us to; we do it because we have taken responsibility for him. Despite my love for him, I am a sinner and an imperfect owner, and he is an animal. There are times when things come up, and he may have to stay in his kennel a little longer or things like that. In his faithless mind, he always knows he will be taken care of. Now think about it, how much more will God, who unconditionally loves you, who is sinless, who is perfect in thought, word, and deed take care of us? He loves us unconditionally with perfect love. He has taken responsibility for us. He is never late and always on time. He has unlimited resources that he makes available to us. I hope we know that we are much more than an animal; we are His children. He has emptied heaven for us, by the way of Jesus Christ. In the darkness we feel, we must always know that God is with us and has taken responsibility for us, and He is no slacker. Our faith is in His ownership of our hands and not our ownership of His. The Bible says, "*The Lord knows those who are his*" (2 Tim *2:19 ESV).* Additionally, we can have faith because the Bible has promised, *"He who began a good work in you will bring it to completion" (Phil 1:6 paraphr).*

Let's get practical. As Christians when we succumb to depression due to a circumstance, we retract to a head knowledge of what Jesus's death did for us on Calvary. The question that comes up is, "Why don't I feel him in this depression?" We say things like, "Look at what I'm going through, where is God?" We must stop focusing on our feelings and focus on Jesus, and His work of the cross. Our faith arises when we focus on Christ, but when we focus on our feelings, feelings smother our faith.

We get the boat syndrome. What I mean is that instead of focusing on Christ out on the water as I spoke about in Chapter 4, we focus on ourselves in the boat. Feelings will have us going back and forth. When we feel spiritually strong, we believe God is close, but when we feel depressed and spiritually weak, we assume God is distant. We let our emotions drive our belief. Then we let our actions dictate our righteousness. Once again, we are not righteous by what we do; we are righteous by whose we are- we belong to Jesus Christ. The amount of faith we have does not determine whether God's promises will be fulfilled in our lives; our faith can be weak or strong depending on how we may be feeling at the time. Instead our trust that God's promises will come to pass is in Christ. Jesus said, *"If I be lifted up, I will draw all men unto me" (John 12:32 paraphr.).* Notice he did not say if we be lifted up, or our circumstance be lifted up. We spend our whole prayer time lifting our circumstance up. We have become professionals at lifting up our circumstances when we should be lifting up God's purpose.

I want to look at another boat experience in another storm. In this account, Jesus was in the boat with his disciples, and the Gospel of Matthew records, *"And when he got into the boat, his disciples followed him. And behold, there arose a great storm on the sea, so that the boat was being swamped by the waves; but he was asleep. And they went and woke him, saying, 'Save us, Lord; we are perishing.' And he said to them, 'Why are you afraid, O you of little faith?' Then he rose and rebuked the winds and the sea, and there was a great calm. And the men marveled, saying, 'What sort of man is this, that even winds and sea obey him?' (Matt 8:23-27*

ESV). Notice that according to this account in Matthew, Jesus first rebuked the disciples' lack of faith before He sought to protect them from what they feared. The disciples spent that whole time focused on the problem even when they had Jesus right there with them. We need to understand something- God is more concerned with His plan and purpose for our lives than He is about our comfort. The best place for those disciples would have been on the side of Jesus sleeping. That would have been a response that would have pleased Jesus. Rowing the boat wouldn't have helped. Work wasn't getting them out of the storm. All of the greats in biblical history encountered life-changing, life-altering storms, but still devastated the kingdom of darkness. Satan will not fight a person or a situation who is not a threat. The greater the storm, the greater the purpose.

Let us also look at the olives on olive trees. In the Middle East, they sit on the branches and look pretty to the observer, but they are of no use until they are plucked and crushed. Once plucked, they are separated from the life-giving tree and the other olives that are like themselves. If we look at this symbolically, consider how we often feel during trials; we can also feel separated and alone. However, once crushed, they are used for anointing oil; the olive now has a purpose. Along with prayer and faith in God, the anointing oil can lead to restoration and healing- the prayer of anyone undergoing trails.

Secondly, we have it even better than the disciples did because while He was beside them, He is in us. He is in our boat even now, and He would ask us the same thing, "Where is your faith?" Is our faith in ourselves or in Him? In Luke's account of this story, He promised them that they would get to the other side, just as in the first storm story. What is your other side? You see, the wind and waves are one thing, but on the other side is the destination. The purpose in the storm is to get to the other side changed. The revelation of Jesus's ability always comes in the boat. The storm forced the disciples to trust in Jesus's purpose while they were in the midst of the storm. Once again, the boat was just the vessel. What vessel is God using to bring you to the other side? Maybe that vessel is a relationship? Is God in that vessel with you changing you and bringing you to your other side? We always talk about the storm, but we leave out the boat. Your vessel could be your job or business; God's plan is for you to use this to help others, and through this He sets His purpose into motion and changing your destiny. Is God in your business? Many are alone in the boat because they refuse Jesus. The disciples, though they could see Jesus, felt alone in the storm. They felt helpless and as if the Lord didn't care. They saw him as silent and asleep. We need to have this revelation- His love is not based on the delivery from the problem, but His presence in the problem. The other side may be heaven for some. Healing will happen on the other side of the storm which may be here on Earth for some or on the other side for others. The faith that they needed was to know that Jesus was with them and protecting them through the storm. Jesus had told them they were going over to the other side. The other side can be provision from a job loss. The other side can be your destiny. The other side can be a healthier view of God through the emotional pain of miscarriage or the death of a child. I want you to hear me very clearly, no matter what you are going through, no matter how dark or deep the pit, no matter how many voices are telling you your circumstance won't change, go to Jesus and go to sleep. Lie beside Him and lock arms. Go rest and trust in His abilities.

The third thing I also want you to consider is what Jesus has done thus far your life. In our storms or despair, we forget all of the past victories He has accomplished for us in our lives. In the pit, circumstances tell us to only look at the here and now. The children of Israel did the same thing. They had to be reminded of the things God did for them in the past. God instructed them to pass down the great things He had done for them to their children. He knew over time they would forget and end up in idolatry. The Psalmist said, "*Bless the Lord, O my soul, and forget not all his benefits, who forgives all your iniquity, who heals all your diseases, who redeems your life from the pit, who crowns you with steadfast love and mercy, who satisfies you with good so that your youth is renewed like the eagle's"(Psalms 103:2-5 ESV).* Don't go to bed fearful or downcast. Go to bed knowing that Jesus is in full control. As David said in verse 4, "*He redeems you from the pit.*" Consider also this verse in Samuel, "*Only fear the Lord and serve him faithfully with all your heart. For consider what great things he has done for you" (1 Sam 12:24 ESV).*

Another thing I want us to consider is that though we can rest in Jesus, we should not let it sideline us from the work of God and cause us to stop working. My dad exemplified this while fighting cancer; despite the diagnosis and despite the treatment, he kept doing the work of the ministry. When we reach out to help others, it refreshes us. The Bible says in Proverbs, "*Those who refresh others will themselves be refreshed" (Proverbs 11:25 NLT).* If we are not careful, feelings will end up dictating our actions; however, it is in the action that purpose and refreshing are carried out. Stagnancy is Satan's anesthesia. In sickness, we need to know that the Holy Spirit does not get sick. He is always willing to move, but we must yield to Him. We may be bed ridden, but the Holy Spirit stills wants to use our voices. Whatever that trouble or sickness may be, God can use us in spite of the hindrance. The Scripture declares, "*But he said to me, 'My grace is sufficient for you, for my power is made perfect in weakness.' Therefore I will boast all the more gladly of my weaknesses, so that the power of Christ may rest upon me. For the sake of Christ, then, I am content with weaknesses, insults, hardships, persecutions, and calamities. For when I am weak, then I am strong" (2 Cor 12:9-10 ESV).* Sickness will take us to the mission field of the sick, the hospital, where they are most primed for the gospel. Both my mom and dad learned this, and this is what enabled them to reach out to those in the hospital in the midst of my dad's chemotherapy treatments.

During a season of feeling overwhelmed or in a time when we may not feel God, this seeming silence does not mean He is silent. Sometimes we just need to adjust our hearing. When we step away from all the other voices, we can hear the still small voice. During our many miscarriages, for instance, even though nothing was changing in the natural, I was growing. That time forced me to dig in and pursue Him. During my dad's cancer despite what I was seeing, I was still trusting in the Lord and believing that He was working in the midst. I experienced Him in both of these circumstances. There can always be a small ember of expectation and faith. It may be locked away, but the Holy Spirit is ready to enrage it. Every day, I wake up and think this is a great day for circumstances to change. We need to keep a level of expectancy because we serve a God who starts at impossible. He can do it. Every miracle Jesus did two thousand years ago in Israel, can be done again in our hometowns. Do you believe? When I read the Bible, I see blind Bartimeus who received His sight. To that I say, Lord, do it again. When I look at the poor woman who suffered from chronic and long-term bleeding, I see her desperation and the pain in her bloodshot eyes. That desperation is no different from what I see many times at the altar. My prayer is "God, do it again." I promise you He can. We don't know what God will do and when He will do it, but He promised He would pour out His spirit, and it is coming. That, my friend, is the hope that I stand on every day for every prayer.

Joy flows from hope. Paul said, *"May the God of hope fill you with all joy and peace in believing, so that by the power of the Holy Spirit you may abound in hope" (Romans 15:13 ESV).* The Bible says that power abounds in hope. What are you hoping and praying for? Is it physical healing? I'm here to tell you to place your hope in God. Is it a mountain that needs to be moved? Jesus said those mountains can be moved and melt like wax. Does your business need a breakthrough? God Almighty is the one who gives us the power to get wealth and influence. He is the Lord of the breakthrough. Paul laid out a simple truth,

"*Rejoice in hope, be patient in tribulation, be constant in prayer" (Romans 12:12 ESV).* These are keys to hold onto when we are waiting for breakthrough to come. Rejoice in hope is to keep a hopeful perception because we serve the God of all hope. Being patient in tribulation is riding out the turbulence while gripping the Lord's hand tightly. It is knowing that there is an end to what we are going through. The key is in the phrase "going through," not staying in the problem. To be constant in prayer is too keep our situation in communication with God at all times. Even if it is not always verbal, we can be in an attitude of prayer about it to God.

Dwell on the times when we shouted for joy and saw mountains melt like wax. We should always desire to function in the joy of the Lord. In that joy, we are moved to action. Happiness is not joy. Happiness can be an outward expression to something good. Circumstances can dictate happiness, but joy comes from God. It is part of who He is. He has given that joy to His children. The Bible says that the joy of the Lord is our strength. That joy comes alive when we worship God through our circumstances. I believe it makes God joyous, and He funnels us His strength. Psalms says, "*The Lord is my strength and my shield; in him my heart trusts, and I am helped; my heart exults, and with my song I give thanks to him. The Lord is the strength of his people; he is the saving refuge of his anointed. Oh, save your people and bless your heritage! Be their shepherd and carry them forever" (Psalms 28:7-9 ESV).* Trust is a settled position or posture that anchors us. Trust in His character and abilities and joy will come. Not because of an immediate fixed outcome, but because of the fueling we receive from the knowing of what is possible. If my trust in God was conditionally based on my desired outcome, then I have nothing more than a genie in a bottle. That is not trust. That is manipulation. It is no different than some of the disciples serving for the purpose of gaining position in the kingdom. The reality is the dungeon of despair has a way of revealing what is in us. When God brings it to light, admit it to Him, confess it and move on. His mercies are new every morning. Let me leave you with one more verse in Hebrews: "*Therefore, do not throw away your confidence, which has a great reward. For you have need of endurance, so that when you have done the will of God, you may receive what was promised" (Heb 10:35-36 NASB).*

Can we pray a faith declaration together?

No matter what season I am in I will choose to remain steadfast in my faith. I will choose to see through the eyes of faith and not feeling. I will monitor my feelings and not be ruled by them. I will grow in my faith as I keep my eyes focused on Jesus and his ability to deliver me. I will keep my ears tuned into that still small voice of God Almighty.

TEN

In the Desert but not Forgotten

And David said to him, "Do not fear, for I will surely show kindness to you for the sake of your father Jonathan, and will restore to you all the land of your grandfather Saul; and you shall eat at my table regularly."
(2 Samuel 9:7 NASB)

For me being childless is like living in Lo-debar. While I do have my step-son Dylan, I define "childless" as not having the experience of raising a child from birth into adulthood. Dylan is now twenty-one-years-old, and he won't let me rock him to sleep. Nor will he watch cartoons with me; remember my earlier attempts. The reality is I move through life missing the fulfillment of my natural desire to be a father to my biological child. You may be saying what is Lo-debar? Lo-debar is the home of Mephibsosheth. It literally translates to a desert place, but it can also be a place that is barren spiritually. I relive this barrenness every time I pass by the little league baseball field or when I walk by the children's section in the stores. We have talked about trials, fiery furnaces, boats, and storms. I pray it has encouraged you; however, you may be wondering about the long lasting battle that has no end in sight. What about the weariness of being left in the desert place? What about that experience that leaves you feeling forgotten? Have you ever cried out to God, "You have abandoned me!" Have you ever lashed out, "You are not coming through when I need you the most!" You may be asking yourself what you will do if your situation never changes. Maybe it is a dream like mine that has not come to pass. Maybe it is a chronic sickness with no cure in sight. I want to tell you that you and I may be in the desert, but we are not forgotten. You and I may feel crippled, but it isn't over yet.

Satan will flood your mind with the same old lies. The ones that say God has forgotten you. The ones that say God cares about everyone else but you. The ones who say God is blessing everyone else but you. Why is that other person getting the promotion over me? Do these sound familiar? What causes you to have these thoughts and to believe these lies when you know they are false? It is the amount of time you have spent in you circumstance without seeing any change. If this is you, you will relate to Mephibosheth. I'll wait as you thank your parents for your name. I still choose to believe that, in spite of your back being against the wall, it is where God is at His best. I do not say this because I have experienced all kind of breakthroughs; I say this because I know that the believing will cause the seeing. I believe God's word. I am sold out to His truth, but I got here from living in the desert. God is our deliverer, and we must preach truth to ourselves and not believe the lies of Satan. He is the God who can make a way where there seems to be no way. He is the God who can make water pour out of a rock. He is the God who sent ravens to feed Elijah. He is the God who fed the widow woman and her son through a prophet. He is the God who shut the mouths of lions for Daniel. He is the ever-present help in the time of trouble. He is our mighty deliverer. He is the conqueror of death, hell, and the grave. His name is Jesus, and He cares for you. God isn't on our side if we have been extra good this week. He isn't on our side because we fasted for 40 days and read the Bible cover to cover 10 times. None of those things qualify us for His favor. We haven't forfeited His favor by not being righteous enough. The common misconception is that when hard times come God has forfeited his favor. I want to share with you the thing that keeps me confident in trust and expectation that God is supernaturally working even though things do not seem to be improving or are even worsening. The key is my relationship with the King, and it's found in the story of Mephibosheth. I'll wait...... I am just kidding.

The story of Mephibosheth is from the book of 2 Samuel. Jonathan, who was the son of King Saul, had a son named Mephibosheth, and when he was five years old he was dropped by a nurse which crippled him. His very name means "the shameful thing." In the story, there are prophetic parallels which means when a story has dual meanings or applications. (Let me give you an example. Joseph in the Old Testament prophetically is a picture of Jesus. Joseph's brothers betrayed him and sold him into slavery. Joseph was falsely accused by Potiphar's wife.

He then ascended to the second most powerful position and was able to deliver those that persecuted him. Does that sound familiar? Jesus was betrayed by his fellow countrymen, and He was sold by Judas for a price of a slave. Jesus was falsely accused. He was crucified, and by His death and resurrection, he has delivered us also. He ascended to the right hand of God and is ruling and reigning as we speak. Another example is in the story of David. David was a shepherd boy who was tending sheep and became the earthly King of Israel. He fought the natural enemy of Israel, Goliath the Philistine, and defeated him. Jesus came as a lowly carpenter's son. He was born in a manger. He is the King of all the Earth and Israel. He defeated the spiritual enemy of the world, Satan, at the cross.) Mephibosheth's story is our own story. At the fall we were dropped to a fallen state by Adam's sin in the garden. Like Mephibosheth, whose fall was not the fault of him but of his nurse, the fall into sin was not our fault but Adam's. Maybe you feel like this right now. Do you feel dropped, so to speak, perhaps even by some action other than your own? Do you feel crippled and unable to function? Perhaps you have fallen to a sickness, or broken dreams, or maybe another loss. Maybe it is the feeling of not being good enough, or perhaps it is your marriage which is in shambles. Whatever your circumstance, you need a miracle. Like Mephibosheth, you are about to be visited by the King who is able to remove you from that desert place. Remember, He fed the three million children of Israel manna every day for forty years. (Someone once calculated how much would be needed to feed them per day, and it would have taken 45 rail cars with 15 tons of manna per cart to meet the need. God did it every single day, not counting the Sabbath. It would have taken 90 cars with 15 tons per car to meet that need.) So let me ask you, "What is your need?" You may be looking at your circumstances. You may have a mountain in front of you and cannot see a way around it. The King is coming. Help is on the way. The enemy will come in and say, " Lo-debar is all there is for you." Isn't it crazy how we hear lies over the truth so loudly causing us to doubt? I have chosen to align myself with God's word on issues I am asking for but not experiencing. The fact of the matter is if my situation doesn't change, I will still let hope rule me. I will still choose to take every thought captive until the day my faith ends in sight. It is our responsibility to capture our thoughts and replace them with truth. How does this work? When you hear the lie, "Nothing will ever change," or "God has forgotten you," we are to take that lie and replace it with the truth. The truth is, *"God is working all things out for my good and His purpose" (Romans 8:28 paraphr.),* and *"The Lord will never leave me nor forsake me" (Hebrews 13:5 paraphr.).*

As I think of Mephibosheth, I picture him just sitting in his crippled condition while everyone else was walking around fulfilling their dreams. It is a picture of the sick watching the healthy run in the park. In my case, it is watching a dad run behind his little girl as he is teaching her to ride a bike for the first time. We can all relate to these types of moments. Do you think it ever crossed his mind that this was all there is to his life? I wonder if he thought, "It is not my fault. I have been placed in circumstances that are out of my control." He, however, did not know about a certain man who was seeking for him. Enter David. After the death of Mephibosheth's grandfather and father, Saul and Jonathan, David became king of Israel. In earlier days, the Bible says that *"Jonathan [had] made a covenant with David, because he loved him as his own soul" (1 Samuel 18:3 ESV).* Jonathan was in a covenant with David; they were in relationship with one another and were best friends. Before I continue, we are talking about a covenant between David and Jonathan that David honored and Mephibosheth benefited from. God has no grandchildren. We are to come into covenant on our own with Jesus, but I want to show you the power of covenant in this regard. Let's proceed. The Bible says, *"And David said, 'Is there still anyone left of the house of Saul, that I may show him kindness for Jonathan's sake?' Now there was a servant of the house of Saul whose name was Ziba, and they called him to David. And the king said to him, 'Are you Ziba?' And he said, 'I am your servant.' And the king said, 'Is there not still someone of the house of Saul, that I may show the kindness of God to him?' Ziba said to the king, 'There is still a son of Jonathan; he is crippled in his feet.' The king said to him, 'Where is he?' And Ziba said to the king, 'He is in the house of Machir the son of Ammiel, at Lo-debar.' Then King David sent and brought him from the house of Machir the son of Ammiel, at Lo-debar" (2 Samuel 9:1-5 ESV).* Little did Mephibosheth know that the king was looking for him because of a covenant made with his father Jonathan. David sent Ziba, which is a picture of the Holy Spirit. The Holy Spirit was sent to us to announce the King. You see- He came looking for you. Jesus said, *"You didn't choose me, but I chose you" (John 15:16 paraphr.).* The Holy Spirit sought me out night after night in the bar rooms. He stayed in the midst of my rebellion constantly drawing and wooing me.

I want you to see that it is about a covenant relationship not a religious experience. It is one that we must enter into with the Lord. The covenant that He made with us with his precious blood was initiated by Him. That covenant also has promises. Those promises apply to you and me. If we are a child of the most high King, we have access to the covenant promises. We must open the Bible and claim them. The Word of God says by His stripes we are healed. It says He will pour out His spirit on all flesh in the last days. His word says He will make a way where there seems to be no way. The Bible says He will be a friend who sticks closer than a brother. This book says He will be our father when our family forsakes us. It says they that wait on the Lord shall renew their strength. This book says our God shall supply all our needs according to the glorious riches in Christ Jesus. This book says He will keep him in perfect peace whose mind is stayed on Him. This book says when we pray believe that we have received whatever we have asked for. He says cast all our cares upon Him for he cares for us. This book says call unto Him and He will show us great and mighty things that we know not. This book says He have given us all authority over all the powers of the enemy. This book says He goes to prepare a place for us, and He will come back and receive us unto Himself and where He is there we will be also. No matter what it looks like, the King is coming back. Are we ready? Our relationship with Jesus is our lifeline in our time of need.

Imagine Mephibosheth's reaction when he heard the

legendary King of Israel was looking for him. We need to remember that potential heirs to the throne were often killed by those in power so as to not pose a threat. Fear may have gripped him. Maybe he thought, "People are looking for me to kill or imprison me because of my grandfather and father." He probably got up out of the dirt feeling even more hopeless for his future. I imagine that he hobbled his way to his closet, put on his best robe, grabbed his crutches, and expected the worst. The Bible says, "*When he came to David, he bowed low to the ground in deep respect. David said, 'Greetings, Mephibosheth' Mephibosheth replied, 'I am your servant'" (2 Samuel 9:6 NLT).* Imagine the scene as he walked into King David's presence. Can you hear the rush of thoughts this man must have had? I am sure he didn't know if his situation was about to get better or worse. Notice, however, that he didn't walk up to David and declare, "I am the child of a king. You owe me." Mephibosheth came up humbly in deep respect. The Bible says, in reverence and awe. That is how we should approach our heavenly king Jesus- in awe and wonder with humility. We can lose sight of that when we have our moments of lament, but when we are frustrated, we must always remember we are talking to a King. To those who don't know Jesus as Lord and are not in covenant, they have to recognize their crippled condition, knowing we are a shameful thing, broken before the Lord of Glory because of the fall, knowing we have sinned. Most people don't realize they are even crippled because they can walk. Mephibosheth utters those words, "I am your servant." Basically he was saying, "I am no threat. I am just so honored to be in your presence, oh King." The reason I make this point is to remind us that we shouldn't get so frustrated with our condition that we lose sight of the honor of being in the King's presence. I don't know about you, but when I tap into the presence of God, I let those frustrations go by the wayside. Like the old hymn "Turn Your Eyes Upon Jesus" says, "Turn your eyes upon Jesus, look full in His wonderful face and the things of this earth will grow strangely dim in the light of his glory and grace." I want to encourage you to get away and get in the King's presence and worship Him for who He is.

Nor did David say, "I'm not helping him. I remember everything Saul put me through." David was merciful; he didn't hold Saul's behavior against the grandson. David was honoring his covenant with Jonathan. We need to know that Jesus feels the same way because of Calvary. He chooses to bless us the very people who were against him- the very people who put him on the cross with our sin.

Some of you may be fearful of the outcome of your situation. Can I just be totally real with you right now? The outcome will be the outcome, but it will be ok because the King is with us. The Bible says, *"And David said to him, '**Do not fear**, for I will surely show kindness to you for the sake of your father Jonathan, and will restore to you all the land of your grandfather Saul; and you shall eat at my table regularly'" (2 Samuel 9:7 NASB).* Jesus is saying this to us, "Do not fear." Our heavenly king sees us. He sees our circumstances, and He sees our tears. He sees and cares because we are His brothers and sisters in covenant with Him. Jesus wants to tell us the same words as He told His disciples when the winds and waves were about to destroy them. He is telling us, "Fear not." His covenant promises are ours, and they apply to us. God shows us kindness for Jesus's sake. We don't deserve it, and we did not earn it. One minute we were like Mephibosheth- hopeless. We feel down and out, helpless, and crippled believing the promises of God don't apply to us because they have not come to pass yet, but the very next moment we are in His presence. No matter where you are, open your ears. Can you hear the King calling for you? Can you just focus on the covenant promises of God and not on the discouragement of the circumstance? Satan uses our circumstance as his megaphone; God uses His word as His megaphone. Fill your mind with His word; fill your soul with His presence every day and wait patiently for him to move. You see, Lo-debar may not be an actual place today, but it is a mindset. At any moment, the precious Holy Spirit can rush into our rooms, and everything can change in an instant. There are things that I don't understand. Has my circumstance changed? As of right now, no they haven't, but my hope has grown tremendously. I want to live and leave a legacy of faith for my family and friends. If I were to walk away, I would lose everything. First and foremost, I would be walking away from my Savior, and without Him, I have nothing. Secondly, I would lose the heavenly reward of reuniting with my children. No matter how disappointed my circumstances get, I still have my Jesus.

Jonathan was a great friend to David, and in the story of Mephibosheth, we see his relationship with David affected his lineage. By our love and commitment to Jesus, we can literally influence our bloodlines from Christ because of our perseverance in the long drawn out battle. This speaks louder than ten thousand sermons to those who are watching us. Our faithfulness to Christ in the midst of the dry places could be the very thing that inspires our future bloodlines to pursue Jesus. Stay focused in the midst of the trial because there is no telling how it is helping the people around you. The end result is that David's relationship with Jonathan changed Jonathan's son's life. He said he could eat at his table for life. So can we, but we can't give up.

One day, the King will restore what we have lost. Listen to these verses: "*Then he* [Mephibosheth] *bowed himself, and said, 'What is your servant, that you should look upon such a dead dog as I?' And the king called to Ziba, Saul's servant, and said to him, 'I have given to your master's son all that belonged to Saul and to all his house. You therefore, and your sons and your servants, shall work the land for him, and you shall bring in the harvest, that your master's son may have food to eat. But Mephibosheth your master's son shall eat bread at my table always'" (2 Samuel 9:8-10 NKJV).* David promised not only to care for his needs but also to restore the land of Mephibosheth's grandfather. Listen, I have lost land here, meaning I have lost lineage here, but beyond the stars my children are at the King's table waiting on their father and mother, never to be separated. I don't know how all these promises play out in the here and now, but they are not empty promises. Some of you are crippled here and still may be after you read this book, but one day we will see every single promise fulfilled in our lives when time as we know it is over.

Much like Mephibosheth, he was still crippled, but he was at the table. What is the message in this? Sometimes, I still walk spiritually through this miscarriage situation on crutches. As Mephibosheth sat at the table with David and his family, they all looked the same from the waist up; however, if we were to look under the table, we would see an obvious difference. I choose to keep my eyes above the table. I am just happy to be dining with the King. Because I am in relationship with Jesus, one day soon the trumpet is going to sound, and the King will come for me. I will be escorted into the third heaven where I will dine at the Marriage Supper of the Lamb. I will leave my crutches of disappointment here. I will sit at the great banquet table on high with my children and that hope keeps me going every day. I do what the book of Titus says to do, I am "*looking for the blessed hope and the appearing of the glory of our great God and Savior, Christ Jesus" (Titus 2:13 NASB).*

I want to also share with you a bonus nugget that the Lord gave me. He convicted me that though I have kept my eyes under the table, I also have to remind myself to stop playing footsies with the Devil in my mind. The temptation in this present life can be to focus under the table, but we need to keep our eyes above the table where we can see Jesus. Let's look at the table from another perspective; let's say that the above the table portion is heaven. We have divided time and declared its end as death, but Jesus sees it differently. He says we have eternal life. In like manner, I view time as under the table and above the table where under the table is what we experience in life, but over the table is eternity. Eternal life is the big picture. It begins at salvation and continues forever. Before Christ, all you and I can see is under the table. To explore this idea further, let's look at these verses in a translation that places eternity in its correct present tense. It is a translation from one of the greatest Greek scholars of our time, Kenneth Wuest. Wuest's Expanded Translation says "*that everyone who places his trust in Him may be having life eternal. For in such a manner did God love the world, insomuch that His Son, the uniquely begotten One, He gave, in order that everyone who places his trust in Him may not perish but* ***may be having*** *life eternal" (John 3:15-16 Wuest Expanded Trans.).* Look at another verse which further expands this idea: "*Truly, truly, I say to you, whoever hears my word and believes him who sent me has eternal life. He does not come into judgment, but has passed from death to life" (John 5:24 ESV).* What I want to drive home to you is that death is not the end. It is the transition from one place to another in the eternal life you have **now**. It is the transition from seeing under the table to above the table. All promises apply, but the timing is what we struggle with because we expect everything here. We focus on the temporary under the table instead of the eternal above the table. We are focused on the 70, 80, or 90 years. Those who aren't healed here are crutch-less there. Those who die here transition to there. Those who experience lack here will receive abundance there, but listen, while you are here, keep seeking, keep learning, and keep trusting because at any moment this thing that has plagued you can turn around. Can I encourage you to keep an eternal perspective and stay focused above the table and stay anchored in the blessed hope? Wait patiently on the promises because they are ours through the covenant we entered into at the cross.

Let us pray a declaration of faith?

Lord, I thank You that I am in covenant with You. I declare that I am grateful to have a place at the table with You, my King. I will resolve to keep my view eternal instead of temporary. I will choose to keep my hope anchored in Your return, and I know that everything will make sense as I choose to keep my focus above the table even in my circumstance.

ELEVEN

A Heavenly Vision

"I know a man in Christ who fourteen years ago-whether in the body I do not know, or out of the body I do not know, God knows-such a man was caught up to the third heaven. And I know how such a man-whether in the body or apart from the body I do not know, God knows-"
(2 Corinthians 12:2-3 NASB)

I want to share something else with you that really caused my heart to heal. Now before I tell you this, you need to know that I am not that guy. I am not the guy who puts a lot of stock in every manifestation that people claim; some of those dreams are the result of late night pizza. I am careful to not be critical of people's experiences, but there are so many things out there. I want the true things of God, not the counterfeit. With that being said, I am not just saying something to sound super-spiritual because once again, I am not that guy. When I tell this I always preface it by telling people that this could just have been a great thought I had, but if it was just a thought, I wish I could conjure this up at will because it brought so much healing to me, and this healing has remained. I never want to say something is of God when it is not because I respect the things of God too much to make a sham of it. I believe in the supernatural abilities of God. I believe in the gifts of the Spirit. I believe what the Bible says about the last days. The book of Acts says,*"And in the last days it shall be, God declares, that I will pour out my Spirit on all flesh, and your sons and your daughters shall prophesy, and your young men shall see visions, and your old men shall dream dreams" (Acts 2:17 ESV).*

I believe that God knows exactly what we need. I quoted all the Scriptures I knew to build my faith in the midst of what I was facing, and there is power in that. I spent hours in prayer during these struggles, and there is power in that also. I also appreciate the experiential times that are gifts of "suddenlies." God gave me a gift on this day that would change my life forever. It was the only time I would experience anything like what I am about to tell you.

During one 9:00 am Sunday morning service, Pastor Todd preached a sermon on God-inspired dreams. During the 11:00 am service, I expected to hear the same message; however, those plans would change as the God showed up mightily in the worship service. As I was worshipping, the worship team sang one of my favorite worship songs about loving the presence of God. Prior to the service, I had crossed paths with what seemed like every pregnant woman on the way to my seat that morning. I was so broken and disappointed. I remember asking God,

"Why can't that be us?" Pastor Todd gave a word of knowledge and that word was that the Lord was going to reveal some things to us in a vision. He said, "God is going to reveal some things to his people. God will show us things if we looked to Him." In my moment of pity and desperation, I heard these words and continued to worship Jesus with my eyes closed. All of a sudden I felt a coolness like a wind blowing across my skin. I had my eyes closed, but I could see a brightness, and it felt as if something had placed two hands covering the sides of my head blocking my peripheral view even though my eyes were closed. The music began to fade. Then I saw a huge column as if it were the entrance to a gate. At the entrance was a man, and instantly I knew He was Jesus although His face was not clearly visible. It's kind of like He was blurred, but in a glorious way. The feeling I felt in His presence is, to this day, indescribable. All I knew at that moment was that I did not want to leave His presence. It was as if a magnet was pulling me to Him. I can also remember that we could communicate without speaking because He could answer my thoughts. I was so broken wanting to express my sorrow to Him, and He knew what I was going to say. It was like a prodigal son moment, and I was trying to get my speech out. I finally began to verbally repent. I said, "Lord, I'm so sorry for letting this come between us." I remember unloading my sorrow and guilt, and He cut me off saying, "I paid for that. It's ok. It's ok." I then asked, "Lord, why?" He didn't tell me why. All He said was, "I wanted it this way." This confused me. Did He want this vision to happen this way? Did he want the miscarriages to happen this way? To this day I still don't understand. He said, "I want to show you something," and as he motioned with His arm, instantly my view was enlarged. Before all I could see was Him in my view; however, as my view expanded, behind Him I saw five shadowy figures. I just knew that they were my children. Their faces were blurred, but I remember making out that they had dark hair and were different heights. I also knew for some reason that they were different sexes. Strangely, I also saw a sixth child who was not part of the group and standing off to the side. Shannon and I had only had five miscarriages at this point. There was a child there who was not part of that group. The next thing I knew, I was with the five of them. I didn't take steps toward them; I was just with them. We began hugging one another, and I still can't describe what I felt, but an overwhelming sense of completion and love filled me as I felt their little bodies and heads against me. Then instantly I was at the throne of God, and I was standing next to a huge step. Suddenly I fell on my face crying and worshipping God. My heart was full of joy and peace. I could hear and feel wind or rushing water all around me, and it was loud. I had a sense of ultimate peace. I knew that there were millions of people around me, yet I felt like I was the only one. The next thing I know it was over, and I could hear the worship music again.

I felt much like what the great Apostle Paul must have when he said, *"Whether in the body or not I do not know?" (2 Corinthians 12:3 paraphr.).* I think he was referring to how real such visions and dreams can feel. I know I never left the auditorium because I was standing next to Shannon the whole time. I also know that from that moment I was changed. I felt whole; I felt gratitude rise up in me to replace the confusion, disappointment and bitterness. However I was very nervous to share it with anyone. I did tell Shannon later that afternoon, and she was blown away. I am not sure that she grasped the experience completely because it was so hard to relay it to her. It is easy to explain the experience in words, but it is impossible to convey the feelings. That afternoon, I mustered up the courage to call Pastor Todd to share what had happened and to ask for some counsel. He listened intently as I explained all I had experienced. He also knows that I am not that guy. The thing that encouraged me to accept the experience as one from God was that everything that had happened lined up with Scripture.

Any time we have an experience, we need to come back to the Scripture and make sure what we experienced aligns with the Word of God. As we talked, we went over every aspect of it and looked at Scripture, and amazingly, I was shocked at what I found. Let me give you some examples of what I am talking about. I couldn't make out the faces because they were glorified. The Bible says, "*For now we see in a mirror dimly, but then face to face. Now I know in part; then I shall know fully, even as I have been fully known" (1 Cor 13:12 ESV)* which explained to me why I could not make out faces because I cannot see clearly in perfect glory. This also explained to me how Jesus could read my thoughts. As I think about being at that huge step or block and I spoke about the sounds I heard, these verses came to mind. In Acts, the Bible says, "*And suddenly there came from heaven a noise like a violent rushing wind, and it filled the whole house where they were sitting" (Acts 2:2 NASB)*. There are also these verses which describe the sound of God's voice: "*The voice of the Lord is upon the waters; The God of glory thunders, The Lord is over many waters. The voice of the Lord is powerful, The voice of the Lord is majestic" (Psalm 29:3-4 NASB); "His voice was like the sound of many waters" (Ezekiel 43:2 NASB); "And I heard a voice from heaven, like the sound of many waters and like the sound of loud thunder" (Rev 14:2 NASB); "Then I heard something like the voice of a great multitude and like the sound of many waters and like the sound of mighty peals of thunder" (Rev 19:6 NASB).* As Pastor Todd and I talked, verse after verse came up to validate my experience, and I believe it also validated the word of knowledge He gave.

Still, there was one part that still troubled me, and it was the child off to the side. I would come to know the explanation for this later, and it really cemented the vision for me. Right before that service, we had gone to another doctor visit with my dad. The latest scan revealed another tumor on his liver; they said my dad would need radiation treatment for it. In my frustration and anger towards God I told him, "So you're going to let a tumor grow and not a child?" Instantly I was pricked in my heart at that statement. I must admit I was going through a lot, and I was looking like an inconsistent Christian. I was on a faith journey that resembled a roller coaster with the seat belt of emotion, and I wanted off. A couple of weeks after that diagnosis and the service where I had that vision, Shannon told me that we needed to talk. She proceeded to tell me that she knew I was going through a lot with my dad, and she didn't want to get my hopes up only to be let down, but she was pregnant and had been for a couple of weeks. We also had a doctor's visit coming up that week for an ultrasound. The vision came to me instantly, as well as the final explanation. I would love to tell you that I brought those cameras into the ultrasound room and amazingly there was a heartbeat, but I would be lying to you. There was no heartbeat for our sixth child. The Bible promises a peace that surpasses all understanding, and it doesn't say once the storm passes or when we get an answer. We ultimately dealt with sorrow once again, but the peace of God was guarding our hearts and mind, and we didn't have to conjure up thoughts to get it. I will also say that the tumor on my dad's liver that was on that scan was rescanned later, and this time it was gone.

TWELVE

Believing in the Season of Weariness

What I always feared has happened to me. What I dreaded has come true.
(Job 3:25 NLT)

What do you do when what you have been doing takes the worst possible turn? You keep on believing, and I can tell you this from experience. Thursday, Feb 18, 2016, was a day that drained the life out of me. It was the day our family felt most like Job when he said, *"The thing I feared came upon me" (Job 3:25 paraphr.)*. On this day, the best doctor in this field at MD Anderson said that there was nothing more that could be done for my dad's cancer. He was going to be sent home to hospice. This is a time when we must come face to face with what we believe. After 11 years of fighting this battle, our faith was stronger than ever. I realize if you preach on faith for healing or miracles, it makes people feel uncomfortable. Many sermons can make it sound like healing or deliverance is based on how the asker responded. For example, some believe that if they have a moment of doubt or if they do not pray with a strong and unshakeable faith, then their prayer will be voided; however, the outcome of a prayer is not always dependent on our human moments and failings. My intent is not to give an answer for what God Himself has not answered. Some things just have no answers. I believe our being able to trust Jesus through the unanswered is the highest level of devotion. Looking at what didn't happen can spawn disappointment. I submit that we need to stay away from the why's and why not's and stick to the Bible. We need to not base our belief system on experience or testimonies, good or bad.

Experience changes perception. Let me give you an example. I was going to make a hospital visit to a lady's brother who attends our church. It was raining on this day, and as I was walking under the overhead drop off area, an elderly man suddenly pulled up in a van. He said, "Excuse me, sir. Would you mind bringing this package to the front desk for me?" I thought he wanted to drop the box off before parking so the box would not get wet. I took the box to the front counter and said, "Excuse me, ma'am, but a man pulled up in a van and asked me to drop this package off to the front desk." She immediately exclaimed, "Oh no, sir! I am not receiving this package from a strange man in a van." Then it hit me! I realized what it looked like, but honestly I was aggravated already because I wasn't having the best day myself. I responded, "Look. I don't have time to go back and forth with you about this. If you won't take this package, then I will just go put it at the door and wait for the man to come in and bring it to you." I then walked over to the door and left this mysterious package at the front sliding door of the hospital. (I know what you are thinking.) As I walked back in front of the front counter and headed for the elevator, I heard her getting on the phone with security. Obviously, this was not looking good for me even though I was innocent. I was just thinking that I wanted to make my visit in case it was something serious, and I really didn't want to be tied up with a misunderstanding. I thought, "I'll just deal with it on my way down." After I visited the gentleman and prayed for him, my heart was racing as I left his room, not sure if I would walk downstairs to guns drawn. I went down the elevator and walked straight to the front desk where the security guard was waiting. I asked if the gentleman had ever come to get his package. He said no, but suggested that we walk over and look at the package. I obliged. As we opened the package, I instantly thought, "What if there is something bad in here?" It will look like I am a terrorist or drug smuggler. I should have known better than to accept the package with all that is going in the world. In the end, the package was only something for a patient who was in the hospital. The guard let me leave once the box was opened, but I didn't stick around to see what was in the box beyond seeing a sheet at the top. For all I knew, there could have been drugs at the bottom. At any rate, I left and listened for my name on the news on the way home. My point is that before the September 11th attacks, the request by this man would have been harmless, but because of that experience, everyone's perception changed.

When we see an experience that didn't pan out like we expected, we shouldn't lose all hope, but come back to the Bible. I am fully aware that many people have experienced shake-ups in their faith because it didn't turn out how it was prayed for. I am one. I know you may have prayed with all of your heart, and yet it still didn't happen like you expected. I want to share with you some things I learned through miscarriages and the sickness of my dad. I learned to isolate my experience. I learned to take every pregnancy and test result on a case by case basis. I would try not to look at the fourth miscarriage and expect it to happen at the fifth one. I would renew my faith for each battle. I kept the experiences separate and tried to not take one disappointment into the next circumstance. I prayed for each situation not looking at the history of the previous circumstance. I did the same thing with my dad's test result. If he had a bad scan before, I would just pray with renewed faith and expect a positive outcome for what was approaching. I think of it as manna from heaven each day; the Israelites had what they needed, so it is the same in faith. Take fresh manna into each situation in each journey. Experience can become worms affecting what the Lord wants to do fresh in each situation. I encourage you to do that in every area of your life, each relationship, each job, each task, and each child. Don't parent a child from a previous experience and hold them to something they have not done. Many times we parent from what we did or experienced and put things on our children that they have no intention of doing or thinking, but in our smothering we create ourselves in them.

I learned to trust in the God who never fails no matter what I deem as failure. I must live for the perfect purpose of God and that is where I learned to keep my focus. I learned to always stay trusting in His word no matter what I see. Faith is believing and standing on God's word, as well as acting on it. Trusting is trusting Him in the outcome. For myself, in regards to miscarriage, I still choose to believe in spite of what I was seeing. In return, it built my faith- rather than discourage my faith- for the impossible. One night, I was praying about this very subject, and the Lord impressed a thought upon me. It was one of those moments when you know you heard from God. I resolved within myself to pray for the miraculous, not because I see the miraculous, but because I believe the miraculous. The believing will cause the seeing. This is the final analysis of what I came up with in that conversation with him: all we can lean on is what we believe, but there should be something in us that causes us to rise up and fight the fight of faith. The resurrecting power of the Holy Spirit causes us to rise up out of a dead situation. This is what He does. He causes us to rise up in situations that seem dead. Faith ends in the sight of receiving what we prayed for; believing in what you have seen or received is not faith. Faith is in the journey, in the process. Many coast when they are winning, but the fight comes when we are on the ropes. We have gotten passive because of what has not happened instead of fueling our faith of what could happen. Each disappointment is a log for when the fire falls. True faith is still believing and not getting derailed no matter what the outcome; true faith is trusting He knows what He is doing. Don't get derailed either in pride if something does happen, or doubt and unbelief if it doesn't happen. Our part is to just believe and step out. If we will hold on in the midst of the season of disappointment, we will see the miraculous, and I declare that by faith.

The Bible says, "*Let us not lose heart in doing good, for in due time we will reap if we do not grow weary" (Galatians 6:9 NASB).* The degree to which we suffer will be the degree to which we receive blessing, if we won't quit. Now when we are going through the fire, do we rise up in faith? I know people say, "Aw sha, look how they are trying to cope." (That is how we say it in South Louisiana.) Our greatest expectation should lay in the most desperate, hopeless situation. Our God is a God who thrives in a hopeless situation; he shines in the darkest of night. He shows up when we have a sea in front of us and an army ready to destroy us behind us. He showed up when Peter was drowning. He showed up for Daniel when the lions were most hungry. He showed up in the midnight hour for Paul and Silas. He was in the furnace waiting on the three Hebrew boys. He did this when it was hopeless, not before they got thrown into the sea, the pit, the jail, and the furnace. My friend, that is where we should be most alert. How we respond to the circumstance reveals what we believe. Do you stay paralyzed in fear, worry, or doubt?

I want to share with you how the Bible reconciles faith for healing in the face of terminal illness. This is where faith becomes real and raw; it is easy to believe in healing in a hypothetical or temporary situation; however, it is an entirely different thing to believe for healing in the face of a terminal or chronic illness. Extending our faith is found in the risk, but in the risk is also the reward of God doing something mightily. Here's the decision: we can let faith rise up like a wave so high and ride it like a surfer or dash against the rocks where the fall is greatest. Many would say the rocks aren't worth the risk. I choose to rise up. I am sharing something with you that I am also preaching to myself and my family. God has done some amazing things in the last 11 years for our family, even while some things did not go as I would have liked them to. I still believe this after 6 miscarriages and my dad's battle. After 11 years of struggling in my faith for miracles, I have come to this conclusion: *"though He slay me, yet will I trust in Him" (Job 13:15 KJV).* I will still choose to believe in my miracle-working, water-walking Savior and His power. Jesus can roll away the stone of broken dreams, disappointments, and resurrect that Lazarus in our lives. I will choose to believe that nothing is impossible to them that believe, no matter what! I've experienced too much. These fires and disappointments are what have caused my faith to grow, not because I have seen positive outcomes. I want to start by sharing this verse in Hebrews: *"For indeed we have had good news preached to us, just as they also; but the word they heard did not profit them, because it was not united by faith in those who heard" (Hebrews 4:2 NASB).* The key of this verse is that everything we hear when reading the Word of God or sitting under teaching of the word will profit us nothing if we don't apply faith to it. For example, although salvation has always been offered to us, we weren't saved until we exhibited faith in His word. The Bible says, "*This is good, and it is pleasing in the sight of God our Savior, who desires all people to be saved and to come to the knowledge of the truth" (1 Timothy 2:3-4 ESV.)* God's desire is His will, so by faith we respond, and without faith, we don't receive the promise of eternal life. God has given us free will to believe, and the reason people perish is not because of God's will, but because they exercise their own will.

I don't want to look at everybody else. I can only deal with me, and you can only deal with you. When we look at these truths in prayer, we must look at them through the eyes of faith, as well as believing and receiving. It only takes you and God. The Word will not profit us if we don't mix it with faith. We understand that. We approach anything in the word by the word not someone's experience or someone's testimony. Testimonies can be encouraging or discouraging. For instance, I have never received a child due to miscarriage, but should I not pray for you who are wanting children because of what I have experienced? On the contrary, it moves me to greater faith for you! Should I believe that miscarriage is the norm? Obviously not, but it is my normal. Should I say, "Yea, I'll pray for you to have a baby, but you should know that we were not able to have one, but come see let me pray." Our barrenness should be the fuel for your breakthrough. God says to ask for the miraculous, not the normal; the normal will happen no matter what. God didn't tell us to narrate the problem; He told us to ask for the impossible, for His power to intervene. The problem is that we are too weary to ask because of our experience. I get that. The

Bible says in Psalms, "*You are the God who performs miracles; you display your power among the peoples" (Psalms 77:14 NIV).* Notice He is not the God who performs the normal. David says He is the God who performs miracles. The book of Job tells us, "*He performs wonders that cannot be fathomed, miracles that cannot be counted" (Job 5:9 NIV).* Do you want someone to pray an "If it be thy will" prayer, or do you want someone to petition our miracle-working Lord for what your need? The woman with the issue of blood didn't say, "Lord, if it be thy will." She came in faith and believed. These people came to Jesus in desperation. Are you desperate enough to push through?

We ask God for what we want or what we need, because that is what He says to do. The Bible says in Hebrews, "*Therefore let us draw near with confidence to the throne of grace, so that we may receive mercy and find grace to help in time of need" (Hebrews 4:16 NASB).* Can you hear Jesus as he asks Bartimaeus, "*'What do you want me to do for you?' Jesus asked him. The blind man said, 'Rabbi, I want to see.' 'Go,' said Jesus, 'your faith has healed you'" (Mark 10:51-52 NIV).* We pray for healing for others. We, as brothers and sisters, should pray in faith rather than follow our prayer with, "I believe, but this one time it didn't turn out." I respond, "Yes, but this one time there was a blind beggar named Bartimaeus who received his sight. One time, there was a leper who was healed. One time, there was a lady with a bleeding issue who was healed. One time, there was a dead man who walked out of a tomb who had been dead four days. One time, there was a man with a legion of demons who was set free. One time, there was a little girl who had been dead, but she rose up. One time, there was a barrel of meal that miraculously stayed full in a famine. One time, there was a raven that fed a prophet. One time, there was a boy who would throw himself into the fire, and he was set free. One time, there was a funeral that Jesus crashed and raised the dead. One time, there was an issue of death, but that got defeated by a water-walking Savior who can walk all over your problem." We should not base our view of healing based on what we did or didn't see happen, but if we want to base our beliefs on a testimony, then the Bible is filled with them.

The opportunity for healing in today's churches are hindered by our disappointments; these often cause us to pray in doubt rather than in faith. Some Christians and denominations do not believe in God's ability to heal supernaturally as we see written in the Bible, and many of these doubts are a result of prayers that did not result in healing. In some cases, healing is seen as only being for those who have the gift of healing, but Jesus gave us a biblical charge to lay hands on the sick and expect them to recover. We are not to be shaken because of defeat or shrink back in the war for sick bodies. How can we declare life while expecting death? Can death happen? Absolutely, but God didn't call us to declare death, He called us to declare life. He didn't call us to narrate the obvious; He called us to believe for the miraculous. He said that He is able to do above and beyond what we think or ask. He said to call on Him, and He will show us great and mighty things. We trust what we see rather than what is unseen, and that is a direct contradiction to the kingdom of God. No one has seen Jesus, yet we have given up everything to follow Him. Faith for miracles is the same. It is not ruled by what we see; it is discovered by what we believe but don't see. The same cross that testifies of salvation also testifies of healing because Jesus took our infirmities, pains, and sicknesses on Calvary. We give Him our sicknesses, and He gives us His healing.

We should not create an "if it be thy will" theology. Instead, we preach and teach the Word to allow people's experience to rise to His word. In the raising of our expectations, we see God move; however, we should not allow our faith to cause us to rebuke people if they don't have the same faith. In the final analysis, we should believe with everything in us, but understand that God is sovereign and the outcome will be based on how He responds, and every situation will look differently. Our faith should be simple because He calls us to believe as if He will. Look at the leper who asked Jesus to cleanse him if it was His will. Jesus said, "I will." Never do we see in the Scripture where He says no, but we see people die of sickness every day. This is the great mystery, but we should not camp out in the unanswered.

We are to be like Jesus, and His mission was given to Him by God. Listen to this verse, "how *God anointed Jesus of Nazareth with the Holy Spirit and with power. He went about doing good and healing all who were oppressed by the devil, for God was with him" (Acts 10:38 ESV).* Jesus sent us to do the same. As He instructed His Disciples, *"All authority in heaven and on earth has been given to me. Go therefore and make disciples of all nations, baptizing them in the name of the Father and of the Son and of the*

Holy Spirit, teaching them to observe all that I have commanded you. And behold, I am with you always, to the end of the age" (Matt 28:18-20 ESV). He said He would be with us just as God was with Him. Listen to our biblical charge in Mark: *"Go into all the world and proclaim the gospel to the whole creation. Whoever believes and is baptized will be saved, but whoever does not believe will be condemned. And these signs will accompany those who believe: in my name they will cast out demons; they will speak in new tongues; they will pick up serpents with their hands; and if they drink any deadly poison, it will not hurt them; they will lay their hands on the sick, and they will recover" (Mark 16:15-18 ESV).* Again listen to this verse in John, *"'As the Father has sent me, even so I am sending you.' And when he had said this, he breathed on them and said to them, 'Receive the Holy Spirit" (John 20:21-22 ESV).* The key here is the same as in Acts 10; the Holy Spirit does the empowering. John's Gospel tells us another narrative from Jesus, *"Truly, truly, I say to you, whoever believes in me will also do the works that I do; and greater works than these will he do, because I am going to the Father. Whatever you ask in my name, this I will do, that the Father may be glorified in the Son. If you ask me anything in my name, I will do it" (John 14:12-14 ESV).* Even though the healer and the raiser of the dead was in their midst, people still died. People will die because of the consequence of the fall, not because of the absence of Jesus. Once again, we are charged to do what Jesus did: love people, reach out to the hurting, share the gospel, and pray for the sick. Like one has said, "He is in management; we are in sales." We are faithful and obedient, and He sovereignly operates through us.

Jesus preached; He taught; He lived the gospel; He healed the sick, He raised the dead. We are called to do the same. I wonder how many bosses are reading this right now? If you are, do you like to hear your employees tell you that something can't be done? To add insult to injury, they report all the reasons why what you told them to do can't be done. Don't you just love that? I am sure your response is something like, "I don't want to hear we can't. Get it done!" If you had a child who was sick, who are you going to ask for prayer? To the guy who prays the "hope so" prayer, or the one who will pray in authority and faith? Listen, it's not hard to have little to no faith. In fact, that comes naturally. We should partner with someone who believes. Rise up and be that person who believes. Remember, I'm preaching to myself also. I know for myself and others, we can look at experience as our basis of expectation instead of God's word. The fact remains that not all get healed here, but we should still pray.

Even in positive testimonies, we can get discouraged. If we hear a positive testimony, and we experience nothing on our own, then we will start to believe God shows favoritism. We should not base our beliefs on positive testimonies either. It can encourage our faith if we let it, but it can also cripple us. In praying about a situation don't look to the right or the left. Look at the Word of God and stand. The Bible says in Proverbs, *"My son, give attention to my words; Incline your ear to my sayings. Do not let them depart from your sight; Keep them in the midst of your heart. For they are life to those who find them And health to all their body" (Proverbs 4:20-22 NASB).* The question remains,

"What should you and I do in a terminal situation?" If you are battling a diagnosis, yes, hear the doctor's report, but also stay attentive to the Word of God. That is a command from God as our plan of action. He says, "Pay attention to my Word." Faith comes from hearing the Word of God; His words are life. Faith does not come by experience; it comes by hearing, believing, and acting on God's word. It is to say, "Yes, I see the diagnosis, but I will choose to seek God about it." It does not mean to deny the diagnosis. My dad said, "I thank you for your report, but I must check with Jesus." The natural diagnosis takes no faith at all; it is what it is. When disease advances beyond medicine, the only room that is left is supernatural. Since disease is part of the curse, we look to what addressed that, and it is the cross of Jesus Christ. That is where our faith and sight should rest. That means whatever the Bible says about what we are going through that is what we believe. It says that by His stripes we are healed; that is what we hear. That is what we sink our teeth into, and that is the great claim we set our stake in, not a death sentence.

We should take the Word of God and find Scriptures that address healing or whatever our need is and sow it in our heart, water it with tears, and let the Son shine on it. Paul asked in Galatians, *"Does he who supplies the Spirit to you and works miracles among you do so by works of the law, or by hearing with faith?" (Galatians 3:5 ESV).* Have faith for the miracle, but trust Jesus for the outcome. Once again, we hear and apply faith to what we hear. I will not back down from truth just because some truths have been abused in the church world. We hear by faith and apply by faith. Listen to these verses: *"All things are possible for one who believes" (Mark 9:23 ESV).* In Matthew's Gospel it says, *"And seeing a fig tree by the wayside, he went to it and found nothing on it but only leaves. And he said to it, "May no fruit ever come from you again!" And the fig tree withered at once. When the disciples saw it, they marveled, saying, "How did the fig tree wither at once?" And Jesus answered them, "Truly, I say to you, if you have faith and do not doubt, you will not only do what has been done to the fig tree, but even if you say to this mountain, 'Be taken up and thrown into the sea,' it will happen. And whatever you ask in prayer, you will receive, if you have faith" (Matthew 21:19-22 ESV).* I believe we can apply this to any mountain we come in contact with, and we can do what this Scripture says we can do because we operate under the authority of Christ. Cancer is a mountain. Financial struggles are a mountain. Relational struggles are a mountain. Anything that is hindering us is a mountain, and that thing can be cast into the sea. We doubt because we keep our eyes on the symptoms. That is understandable, but we are called to believe what the Bible says. You see, we need a gauge to come back to in the battle of faith. We go through these prayer battles like a ship in the night, but we always veer back to the lighthouse of God's word.

Many, including myself, can tend to get discouraged when we don't see things turn out like we pray for. I don't know about you, but it lights an indigenous fire to push beyond the natural, regardless of what I see or how it has turned out in the past. The book of James says, *"The effective prayer of a righteous man can accomplish much" (James 5:16 NASB).*

Effectual and fervent prayer is where we get the word *energy* from. Energy is strength and vitality, and it is required for long-lasting, physical or mental activity. So what this verse is saying is that an energetic, passionate, heartfelt prayer will produce results. I get that fuel from disappointments, so that is why we should turn our disappointments into fuel for heartfelt, energetic prayers. Seeing someone suffer should not cower us down, but rise us up in compassion to engage. This is why I say weariness is sapping our energy and fervency. This is what it can look like in a real life situation. When a person receives a terminal diagnosis, they share the news with other believers in the church hoping of an all-out war against that diagnosis, but instead they receive, " Lord, give this person strength to endure this thorn in the flesh," or "Oh Lord, if it be thy will, can you please hear this prayer and heal so and so?" All the while this is rooted in fear, doubt, and unbelief of the outcome that we don't get to determine. The Lord said, "I have given you the authority to bind and loose. I have given you all authority over all the powers of the enemy. I have given you My name, My power, My blood; use it." I am just called to believe and act. It is God who determines the outcome. I also understand not wanting to get their hopes up, but I think of it as getting their faith up, and that pleases God. What harm is it in standing with someone to be healed and helping them push through in their faith? It helps them persevere in hope and expectation. It also helps those who are walking through it with them to stay prayed up. For the caregiver, it also helps them process and endure. When all is said and done, don't you want to be able to say I stood until the end and left no prayer unprayed? Without faith, we don't please God. Imagine for a second, a husband and wife who are going through a difficult situation that could destroy their marriage praying, "Oh Lord, whether we make it or fail, let your will be done." That mentality is doomed for failure.

We must pray with determination. The book of James says, "*But he must ask in faith without any doubting, for the one who doubts is like the surf of the sea, driven and tossed by the wind. For that man ought not to expect that he will receive anything from the Lord" (James 1:6-7 NASB).* Other translations say that we ask in faith without wavering. To waver means to be at variance with one's self, hesitant, or doubt. I say that because doubting comes naturally. Believing is the fight, but we believe through the circumstance into the final word from God. That once again is true faith, believing when we see no evidence of change, and then the willingness to accept whatever the Lord does. When we see no evidence of obedience in our rebellious children changing, we should not doubt but instead rise even more focused. When we witness the sickness worsening, we should not stay attentive to the symptoms but instead attend to the Word of God. We dig deeper and call on the God who says to come boldly to the throne and ask for what we need. We come to the one who beckons us to ask, seek, and knock. Keep knocking and knocking, and don't quit no matter what we see. The Bible says in Jeremiah, *"Call to Me and I will answer you, and I will tell you great and mighty things, which you do not know" (Jeremiah 33:3 NASB).* I'm telling you this because we need to come out of our weariness and faithlessness. People are counting on us, the Church, to rise up when they can't. We are still the most powerful organization on this planet. We are the ambassadors of the kingdom of heaven.

There was an extreme approach that derailed people's faith in the 1980's and 1990's; they would not even acknowledge a problem or sickness because they said that doing so and praying for it was "claiming the problem" and the Christian had overcome these already. Now the children of this generation are grown and are sitting on the other side with a bad taste in their mouth wallowing in unbelief and doubt, but somewhere in the middle is God's approach. I think the middle ground is to believe in healing, but accept the final outcome. How can you mentally determine the outcome of a situation and divvy up who will get healed and who will pass on and receive the final healing? Listen, this will help you: As powerful as God is He will not answer a prayer that is not prayed. Yes, He knows our need, but He is waiting on us to ask Him. The problem is people have gotten lazy and just expect God to do things. If people can't come to a believer who believes, then who can they go to? We need to be the first line of defense and the last line of defense in the battle for those around us. There is a barrage of unbelief and doubt that is wearing out the saints of God. Can I challenge to rise up, man or woman of God, and join arm and arm with the family of God and have each other's back? We need to get back to believing His word, and stop focusing on what we are not seeing.

I have been reading the stories of mighty men of old who were part of great moves of God, and they all had the same denominator which was unwavering faith in the sight of sure defeat. I really believe God is disappointed in the image we have created of Him because of the spiritual climate in the United States. Listen, we need to rise up and believe in the God of Abraham, Isaac, and Jacob. When that phrase was uttered in the Old Testament, it meant something and demons ran for the hills. The enemies of Israel ran in all directions. In the New Testament, demons fell at the feet of Jesus whenever they were in his presence and begged Him for mercy. But now, demon spirits come and pull a chair up next to us. This ought not to be. Everyone is watching the Church to see how she responds when our backs are against the wall. We need to rise up in the name of our Savior and show them how powerful and life-changing our God is.

I have made a decision to not focus my eyes only on the natural. Just because I can't see something or hear something doesn't mean I don't believe it is possible. Let me ask you a question, "Do you believe in the rapture of the Church?" If you would say no, then, "Do you believe in the resurrection of the dead?" It is the same event. At any rate, that event is on the horizon, but in the natural it is impossible to participate in that event. It is impossible to float through the sky. It defies gravity, and my eyes would be blinded by His glory in the natural. My ears would explode by a heavenly trumpet blast. There is no telling what decibel range that is! It is also physically impossible to go into and beyond space into the third heaven without disintegrating, especially without a space suit on at least. I believe it, not because I have experienced it or because I can make sense of the natural aspects of it; I believe it because God's word promises it. I am not called to figure it out; I am called to believe. In the same way, I don't know how God drowned an entire Egyptian army. I can't explain manna from heaven. I can't explain how a lions' den became a furniture store for Daniel. All I can tell you is we serve a supernatural God.

The only thing we need in this life is the cross of Jesus, and by this, I mean what He accomplished there. It always has been and always will be. He defeated the sin problem, but He also addressed sickness. Look at this Old Testament story. It is a type and shadow of what Jesus would do. The book of Numbers records this: "*The Lord sent fiery serpents among the people and they bit the people, so that many people of Israel died. So the people came to Moses and said, 'We have sinned, because we have spoken against the Lord and you; intercede with the Lord, that He may remove the serpents from us.' And Moses interceded for the people. Then the Lord said to Moses, 'Make a fiery serpent, and set it on a standard; and it shall come about, that everyone who is bitten, when he looks at it, he shall live.' And Moses made a bronze serpent and set it on the standard; and it came about, that if a serpent bit any man, when he looked to the bronze serpent, he lived" (Numbers 21:6-9 NASB).* We spoke earlier about paying attention to God's word. These verses illustrate the same principle; in verse 8, they are told to look at the serpent on the pole. This is no coincidence. Everything God does is done for a reason. This is a perfect type and shadow of the atonement of Christ that happened at the cross. Healing is in the atonement because the Bible says that He bore our iniquities and disease. The Israelites were murmuring against Moses their pastor, so God sent snakes to bite them. How's that for dealing with rebellion? They came and repented and were healed. Jesus is never referred to as a serpent, but here is a mention of a serpent being lifted up on a brass pole. The very thing that was killing them was the very thing that would save them. The serpent here was sin and sickness that was put on the pole that represented exactly what Jesus would do. A serpent is always represented as Satan or evil. Jesus took on the sickness and sin as an offering on our behalf. We gave Him our sin and sickness, and when we look on him we receive His redemption and healing. In the Old Testament, when the Jewish people had to bring a lamb and sacrifice it for their sin, the lamb didn't become a sinner; it became an offering for the sin of the person. The sin was transferred to the animal and that person walked away covered by what it represented. It was a picture of what Jesus would do for us.

This is not my opinion; Jesus himself said this was a picture of Himself. The book of John records the words of Jesus: *"As Moses lifted up the serpent in the wilderness, even so must the Son of Man be lifted up; that whoever believes may in Him have eternal life" (John 3:14-15 NASB).* The cross is the reason we can expect a miracle. Remember, God instructed Moses to tell the people that when they were bitten by the snakes to look at the serpent on the pole, and they would live. The fiery serpent was killing them. The one on the pole was healing them. The point is that they were looking to the cross to save them from the very thing that was destroying them.

What about when symptoms are testifying against you?

Believe anyway and trust Jesus for the outcome. Remember Abraham and Sarah who were too old to have children? When I was teaching Sunday School years ago, our class did a verse by verse study of Romans. In chapter 4 of that great book, Paul addresses Abraham and how he stayed strong in his faith even though he recognized his body was failing at 100 years old. It is safe to say that at age there was plenty to be discouraged about. Abraham did not trust in his body. His body was telling him there wasn't any way he could have a baby, but he kept trusting in the Lord and was fully convinced the Lord could come through and give him a child. God promised him and Sarah a child, and Abraham stood on that. Did he see the symptoms? Yes, as would be obvious, but he kept his faith in the word God gave him. Allow me to summarize Romans 4: 20-24 for you: God accounted Abraham's faith as righteousness, because he kept his focus on God's word, not on the natural. Then it tells us that it was also written for us, too. I am not saying we don't acknowledge the symptoms; we just don't put our full trust in them. We anchor it in God's word.

Similarily, we can stay focused on what is happening in the natural and that is a realistic view. That is real, but we also have a choice to dwell on what God says about our circumstances in spite of our symptoms. I suggest finding a fellow believer and linking up with them. As Jesus said in Matthew's Gospel, *"Again I say to you, that if two of you agree on earth about anything that they may ask, it shall be done for them by My Father who is in heaven" (Matt 18:19 NASB).*

Let me link up with you right now in a prayer of faith.

Lord, we come boldly to the throne of grace during our time of need. Lord, I join my faith together with the one reading this right now, and I pray in the name of Jesus that every symptom and sickness must bow the knee to our Lord and Savior Jesus Christ. We choose to acknowledge your work on the cross and the fact that you defeated every sickness two thousand years ago on our behalf. I declare by faith that healing is taking place and that every symptom must cease under the authority of the name of Jesus the one who crushed disease.

THIRTEEN

My Greatest Fear Met With Greatest Grace

"O death, where is your victory? O death, where is your sting?"
(1 Corinthians 15:55 ESV)

As I write this final chapter, my heart is filled with awestruck wonder at God's grace. I began this book several years ago, and in the process, many things have happened. In many ways, this book has become a diary of what I have learned throughout the journey. It has also been therapeutic for me. As I write this closing chapter, my hero, my best friend, my dad has died. In March 2016, he left his boat and crossed over to the other side. His testimony was truly a testament that the anchor holds. Today is Wednesday, August 3, 2016. I can tell you firsthand this chapter was birthed out of the worst days of my life, but I think what I learned may help you. In February 2016, Pastor Todd scheduled me to preach a sermon in our latest series a month later in March 2016. As I saw this date on the calendar,

I began to prepare a message that I would have to live out less than a month later. We were in a series at our church about the identity and characteristics of Jesus. Some of the sermons had focused on Jesus as God and Man, His early years, His relationship to the Holy Spirit, His mission on this Earth, and finally His finished work on the cross. We then continued with His resurrection which was the message preached on the weekend my dad died. When it was my turn to preach a sermon in the series, we chose a message on what His resurrection means to us.

As I prepared, I began to reflect on the week before my dad passed away. It was the Passion Week which we celebrate right before Easter. Nathan Sam, one of the greatest worship leaders I have ever known and worship leader at my church, is a dear and personal friend. During the months before my dad's passing, Nathan and my dad had grown really close. Nathan and my dad planned for my dad to sing at a special Passion Week service. Remember my dad had taught me many valuable lessons about serving God consistently in the midst of his 11-year battle with cancer. He was consistent to his family and in ministry, and he loved to sing for the Lord. I will never forget one of the last things my father told me shortly before he passed; he said, "I have tried to show you many things, but the last thing I want to show you is how to die a Christian man." That is exactly what he did. Miraculously, he really only began to look sick a couple of weeks before his passing. I could see him going down quickly during the last two weeks of his life. He began to have to use a cane as his strength was giving out almost daily, but he was focused on glorifying the Lord in every way. On March 13, 2016, a week before my father died and the beginning of Passion Week, I witnessed my proudest moment with my dad. On that Sunday, he sang "Feel the Nails" at both of our church's services. Before then when he had sung in smaller churches, he had always sung along to a disc, but this day would be different for him. On this Sunday, he climbed the platform without a cane, and with all the strength he could muster stood with a full band and a choir behind him. He stood up in front of our church of over a thousand people and uttered the words, "I love Jesus. He's my man." His voice was very feeble the entire last month of his life, and it was extremely feeble during rehearsal the night before; however, when he put that microphone to his mouth that morning, the anointing of the Holy Spirit fell in our midst as he belted out that song with power and beauty. We were in awe as we had witnessed the sustaining power of Jesus Christ in those services. He received a standing ovation, and I knew that it meant the world to him. For him to come to the end of his life and ministry and to finish the race with visible appreciation was a blessing. The applause was not merely appreciation for the song; it was appreciation of a battle-tested warrior of Christ finishing his course strong that inspired us all. I have watched that service over and over again on our church's Facebook page, and I am so proud of what the Lord did through Him. His strength never recovered from that day, and he passed away a week later. In a sense, he left all the Lord had given him on that platform. What a legacy!

Larry Segura (my dad)

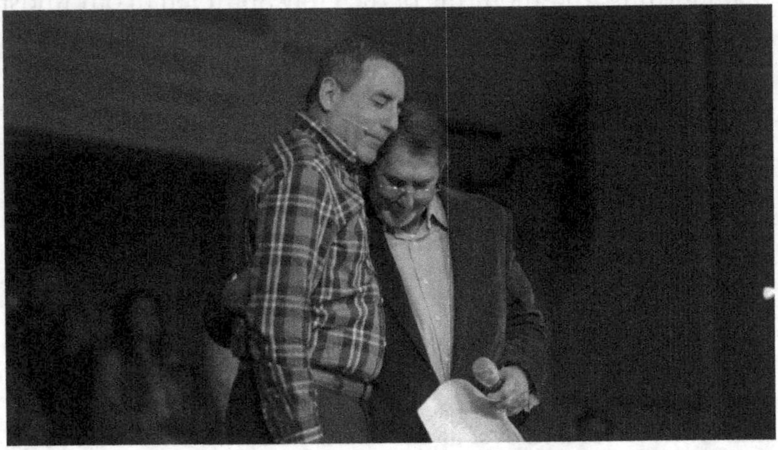

Pastor Todd and my dad

My dad with Nathan in the background

Carol Segura (My Mom) and my dad before he died

Think of the disciples as they followed Jesus for over three years; they saw Him heal sick bodies, raise the dead, cast out devils, and walk on water. Imagine the power of His words that calmed raging seas. On Golgotha's Hill, the man who had spoken life and raised the dead with His words now hung on a rugged cross lifeless. His followers dispersed hiding for dear life. They believed that the new way of life they had dreamed of for three years was over. They felt the promises they received would never come to pass- their hopes dashed with a new reality. I am sure they felt despondent and betrayed; you may even feel that way right now. You, much like, me prayed and had such hope that it was going to turn out like you expected, only to wake up and everything was turned upside down. Now your life looks totally different. Ever felt like that? Maybe you have had devastating situations and you are confused on how to view that circumstance. Do you feel that in your frustration you have blown your relationship with God because of the things you have said or done? Maybe you feel you blew it with the way you reacted when you didn't get your way. You may be saying, "That last chapter didn't work out for you, did it, Kelly?" I think it is once again a matter of perspective. Let me try to explain.

I want to look at some truths I have discovered about the resurrection and how it affects us today practically, spiritually and futuristically. Remember, the disciples gave up everything to follow Him. Now as they saw the sun set before the Sabbath no doubt their dreams and hopes did the same. Have you ever been thrust into a situation and suddenly nothing makes sense anymore? Jesus built the hope and expectation for an abundant life, but instead as they watched Christ die on the cross, they became social outcasts who began living in fear for their lives. They totally abandoned the mission and went back to fishing.

The resurrection was and is an event, but is also a person. When Martha was distraught over her brother Lazarus's death, Jesus told her, *"I am the resurrection and the life; he who believes in Me shall live even if he dies, and everyone who lives and believes in Me shall never die. Do you believe this?" (John 11:25-26 NASB).* Jesus is the resurrection and the life. This one verse tells us that He is our resurrection in both our life and in our death. No matter what appears dead in our life and what appears hopeless, He is our resurrection in each and every one of those life situations. Our lives can be resurrected here on this Earth, as well as futuristically.

Another truth I want to share is that sometimes darkness and earthquakes precede resurrections. Mark's gospel records, "*Very early on the first day of the week, just after sunrise, they were on their way to the tomb and they asked each other, 'Who will roll the stone away from the entrance of the tomb?'" (Mark 16:2-3 NIV).* Early on the third day after Jesus's death, three women Mary Magadelene, Mary the mother of James the less who was one of the disciples, and Salome who was the mother of James and John the sons of Zebedee and also disciples were on their way to the tomb to anoint Jesus's body. It was an honor done in sorrow and pity with a desire to honor the Lord's body. Their only question was who would roll the stone away. Listen, it is the same question we ask today, but worded differently. Today, it may sound like this: "How will this heavy problem be solved because it is too big to move?" or "Nothing in me is able to deal with this situation; it is too heavy. Yet, I need it to move so I can do what I need to do," or even "How will I break the cycle of this addiction?" Friend, Jesus Christ can take any addiction and crush it to powder. Maybe you have said, "I will never get over this." You see for them they endured the suffering of watching Jesus die, and if that wasn't enough that stone was a reminder of their hopelessness. Maybe your marriage has a huge stone that is insurmountable, and it must be dealt with before you can begin the important work on the inside? Maybe it is the stone of unforgiveness that has you in the tomb sealed in misery. Maybe you would say my child has too many negative influences in his or her life, and it is a stone blocking their potential. Maybe it is a sickness that is worsening. Maybe our economy is a stone that has your hopes and dreams sealed in a tomb of despair. Listen, the cross has empowered us to deal with it, and the resurrection gives us the proof that God can resurrect that situation that looks helpless. Jesus is the resurrection and the life.

Catch this- in the middle of the cross and the resurrection were two earthquakes. Sometimes it takes an earthquake to appreciate the resurrection. The book of Matthew says, "*There was a violent earthquake, for an angel of the Lord came down from heaven and, going to the tomb, rolled back the stone and sat on it" (Matthew 28:2 NIV).* That earthquake of devastation that you felt may be the stone that rolled away the problem in your favor. Let's look back for a moment. Earthquakes affect all within its path. When Jesus died on Calvary's cross, there was an earthquake and darkness filled the land. That caused fear and panic, as well as uncertainty. The Bible says in Matthew, *"And behold, the veil of the temple was torn in two from top to bottom, and the earth shook; and the rocks were split" (Matthew 27:51 NASB).* When that darkness covered the Earth, it was the transition of our darkness onto Christ. When the Earth quaked no matter how bad it looked or seemed, it revealed access to God Almighty. In our greatest turmoil, God lays out the red carpet into His presence, but unfortunately, that is when we run the farthest away. You see, the purpose of that earthquake was to reveal the invitation into His presence. That earthquake transpired during the death for Jesus, but it was the transition of access of life for us. You see, friend, if we can keep our composure during devastation we would know where to run. The purpose of the earthquake was to rip the veil; it opened thousands of years of denied access in an instant. Sometimes earthquakes in our lives are intentional to bring about a deliverance that cannot be attained by human hands.

The Bible says that in the last days anything that can be shaken will be shaken, but its purpose is to show what will stand firm and that is the kingdom of God. The book of Hebrews says it like this, *"Once again I will shake not only the earth but the heavens also. This means that all of creation will be shaken and removed, so that only unshakable things will remain.* ***Since we are receiving a kingdom that is unshakable****" (Hebrews 12:26-28 NLT).* In the devastation of my dad's passing, we received peace which comes from the King of Peace who rules a heavenly kingdom that cannot be shaken. Devastation positions us to receive the unshakeable provisions of God. That peace was transferred because of the darkness that was transferred at Calvary so we can have any benefit of the kingdom we need at the moment we need it. Earthquakes in our lives cause others to recognize Christ in our situation and the firmness of the kingdom of God. How many times have I heard in passing, especially at my dad's funeral, "I can't get over how well they are holding up during the service"? Peace in devastation is inspiring because it shows the power of Jesus's ability to keep us in perfect peace if our minds are on him.

Let's continue with the story. The Bible says, "*Now the centurion, and those who were with him keeping guard over Jesus, when they saw the earthquake and the things that were happening, became very frightened and said, 'Truly this was the Son of God!'*" *(Matt 27:54 NASB).* The extreme trials bring an invitation to change. Sometimes it takes some to go to jail to see their purpose, or it takes the devastation of a car wreck to see the need for deliverance from substance abuse. My dad's battle caused everyone's faith to rise through his perseverance in the fight, not the earthly healing from cancer. The grace on my family during this time has been supernatural. I should be in a coma of grief, but God has provided what we need, and it's unshakeable. In the times we are living in right now, we need to learn perseverance in the problem instead of deliverance from the problem. If my dad never got cancer his impact would not have been as great. Jesus used this cancer to get my family to the other side stronger and to preserve our faith. Sometimes we don't get to choose our legacy. Our response to life defines, creates, and cements it. It just happens in our small steps of obedience during battles.

Don't look at the earthquake in your life; look for the messenger sitting solidly on the stone that cannot be shaken. The Bible tells us in Matthew, "*Suddenly there was a great earthquake! For an angel of the Lord came down from heaven, rolled aside the stone, and sat on it. Then the angel spoke to the women. 'Don't be afraid!' he said. 'I know you are looking for Jesus, who was crucified. He isn't here! He is risen from the dead, just as he said would happen'" (Matthew 28:2, 5-6 NLT).* The messenger was there to deliver them a message that the source of their grief had been resurrected. Satan wants us to keep our eyes on the cracks and the broken ground, not on the message. He wants us to assess the damage and not the access to God that has been granted. In fact, he wants us to blame God for the earthquake and run in the other direction. As children of God, if we experience an earthquake of devastation, we should look for the message in it. On Earth, in any capacity as a child of God, the only position to take is that no matter what this devastation looks like, no matter how it is perceived by ourselves and others, we can and should expect a purposeful outcome. The Bible says, "*And we know that God causes all things to work together for good to those who love God, to those who are called according to His purpose" (Romans 8:28 NASB).* The purpose of both of those earthquakes was to let them into His plan and purpose. Those earthquakes created a pathway into His presence. I said all that to say that these ladies came perceiving a situation but the resurrection of hope sprang up in an instant and changed their grief into a message. Sometimes the earthquakes in our lives can bring about the revelation we need to continue. The result of that earthquake gave them the good news that would help the others who were dealing with the same loss. I know some of you reading this book have been through the wringer, but I believe you are a battle-tested warrior. I believe advice and counseling will come through you for those who are crippled by the same things you survived. I don't know what you are dealing with, but God will use it to minister to others to give them hope when they face what you have faced. There was an earthquake at the cross that brought victory. There was an earthquake that brought a resurrection of hope and life.

Let's move on to another post-resurrection appearance, shall we? Here is another truth I learned from Jesus's post resurrection. The resurrection brings revelation on our road of confusion. The Bible says in Luke, "*And behold, two of them were going that very day to a village named Emmaus, which was about seven miles from Jerusalem. And they were conversing with each other about all these things which had taken place. And it came about that while they were conversing and discussing, Jesus Himself approached, and began traveling with them. But their eyes were prevented from recognizing Him. And He said to them, 'What are these words that you are exchanging with one another as you are walking?' And they stood still, looking sad" (Luke 24:13-17 NASB).* According to the text, they were going back and forth with intense emotion as they were searching for answers. What they were encountering now contradicted what they had experienced for the last three and a half years. These experiences weren't aligning with their previous experiences or the Word. There was frustration because what they were reading because it didn't make sense. For instance, I'm sure they were going over what Jesus had said and relating it to the Scripture. The illumination of Jesus was veiled so they didn't see the reason in their pain. In other words, they may have known the Levitical laws and the deliverance with Moses and the promises from Abraham but never connected the plan of Christ in these stories. They never saw Christ as the Deliverer or as the sacrifice who would remain on the altar. They didn't understand the spiritual application to their pain.

Like us today, if we focus on anything we are going through at the surface level, we will stay discouraged. They were distraught that their Messiah had not seemed to come through. Have you ever felt that way? One of my best friends Jeremy and I did this same thing in my driveway one of the nights before my dad died. We were searching for answers to what we had been walking through. We were talking about faith and healing for my dad. Like you, we were searching for reasons and getting hung up on the mysteries; it can certainly derail us. These followers of Christ were doing the same. Luke was saying that they were literally going back and forth trying to process. It was like my conversation with Jeremy. Why do some get healed and some don't even though each believe? It is comparing expectations with reality, in my case, as well as these men on the road to Emmaus. I had this revelation: measuring your expectation against reality without purpose will never make sense. Purpose can only be decided by God. We don't get to decide, but we get to be a part. It is something we do. It is equivalent to: "Why would a loving God allow…?" The men were throwing out theories of why it hadn't work out like they expected. Can we relate to these discussions? We get devastated by something in our life, like I said earlier, and we go to the Word, but it doesn't make sense to us. We read verses that seem to be an obvious fit and immediately claim that promise; however, we are looking only with our eyes and not necessarily God's plan. The fact of the matter is in verse16 it says that their eyes were prevented from seeing Him. For instance in my dad's case, if I get hung up on cancer and suffering for 11 years, I miss the lives he touched throughout the process. If I'm focused on the surface of what is going on my eyes are veiled even though Jesus is walking beside us on the road.

Listen to me, I am so proud of my dad for what he endured, for the lives he touched, and what he taught me. His funeral was the most powerful thing I have ever seen in that regard. My dad brought restoration in his death to all relationships that were shaky at one time. Healing took place on a grand scale that would have never happened if it wasn't for this road we traveled. I saw everyone who was important to us despite our differences- denominations, family, friends, and beliefs- worshipping the Lord with one voice. To be honest, sometimes even though we know what the Lord is doing in a situation, we would still prefer him to do it our way. In this case, the Lord's will was more beautiful than I could imagine. Focusing on what we expect will always cause the veiling, but accepting His plan and purpose will always unveil Him.

Everything we face should have the backdrop of Jesus. That is where the perceiving can happen, simply because it is filtered through His will, plan, and purpose which is perfect. I think when we get so hung up on the details, it masks us from seeing Jesus in our circumstance. Remember, Jesus was discussing what would take place with His death and resurrection, and Peter was seeing it and processing it naturally without seeing Christ as Savior. He didn't understand the magnitude of why death was the only way. All Peter saw was that his best friend was going to die and that wasn't going to happen on his watch. Jesus would constantly say they needed eyes to see and ears to hear. "Eyes to see" refers to seeing God's purpose and plan. In other words, "Peter, if I don't die for you and for those who come after you, you go to hell." These men who had followed Jesus all this time still did not understand the plan and purpose of what Jesus was doing. I think of my dad and the resurrection of faith that I have seen in our family and friends during our most trying time; it caused many to see Jesus as a constant sustaining power. Many became closer to God, and others have come to know Him. Watching him on the platform at Family Life Church as a dying man declaring the power and faithfulness of God was one of the most powerful things I have ever seen. Hearing the words, "I love Jesus; he's my man," will forever be burned in my mind and etched in my heart. The video of his last time singing has gotten over 5,000 views on our church's social media page. To me, the resurrection is the Holy Spirit's power that is available as Jesus's omnipresent ability to open our eyes in the midst of what we are going through. Not only that but to appreciate His presence on the road of confusion.

Let's get back to the account as we pick up the story in Luke 24. The Bible says, "*Then one of them, named Cleopas, answered him, 'Are you the only visitor to Jerusalem who does not know the things that have happened there in these days?'"* (*Luke 24:18 ESV*). If anyone knew of the suffering that had taken place it was the one to which they were speaking. We get to a point where we even think Jesus doesn't understand suffering. To go a step further, Satan, the master deceiver, will tell us Jesus is causing our suffering, when He is the very one who took your suffering. Satan does this to isolate us and to devour our faith and our sanity. Remember, he comes to steal kill and destroy. His plan is to suffocate us with grief and to pulverize us in the ground. His plan is to cut us off from our only hope which is Christ. He wants to make Him the enemy which will cause us to harden our hearts, walk away from God, and separate ourselves to the place called Hell. Our greatest capacity to process disappointment and hurt is in Jesus. He's the one who understands and yet that is who Satan wants to push us away from. Jesus has no hindrance to understanding our weakness and pain. We process it in Christ, not as the cause, but the healer. He is able to help because He doesn't have even a semblance of a hard heart. His heart is pure and undefiled which gives Him the ability to truly bear witness in our greatest pain. Not only can He bear witness, but He can sympathize and take it. His desire is to also give us joy in its place. I choose to keep my eyes above the table in a heavenly perspective. For instance, I see my dad surrounded by all his children and grandchildren right now suffocating him with love instead of him gasping for air on that Saturday morning he passed. God's grace was also great in that moment. After my dad sang that special song on that Sunday, he was in the bed by Wednesday. He would never leave that bed again. On Friday afternoon, he told my mom, "Ok Carol, it's time to get ready to go." He had trouble breathing a bit for about an hour, and the following morning he soared through the clouds to mansions on high in the presence of Jesus Christ. I will say just like I prayed for the children we miscarried to be raised from the dead, I did the same thing when everyone left the room. Then I thought he would be pretty upset if he came back so I stopped. Knowing he is with our family in the portals of glory fills me with joy unspeakable. Because Jesus resurrected, we know we will be also, as well as all who know Christ. The resurrection means we can have a resurrected perspective in our greatest trial.

Jesus can't fail, Everything He does is perfect so we never lose, but we must see Him in it. Jesus then asks Cleopas (one of the men walking to Emmaus and talking with Jesus) to explain these things, and he does. Cleopas describes the events, and it reveals his expectations of how he thinks things should have worked out. His expectation was masking the true meaning of what had happened. I want to pause here and look at what they were missing. They lacked the spiritual purpose of the situation. They were mourning their loss and how they felt it should have worked out, and it was that very thing that blinded them from seeing Jesus. Jesus was patient with them, and the

Bible says began to explain the Scriptures to them. Luke tells us, "*And he said to them, 'O foolish ones, and slow of heart to believe all that the prophets have spoken! Was it not necessary that the Christ should suffer these things and enter into his glory?' And beginning with Moses and all the Prophets, he interpreted to them in all the Scriptures the things concerning himself*" *(Luke 24:25-27 ESV)*. Jesus was showing them the purpose of the pain they were experiencing. That's what we have to understand. There is always a purpose in what we face; it is never pointless. The Bible says, "*So they drew near to the village to which they were going. He acted as if he were going farther, but they urged him strongly, saying, 'Stay with us, for it is toward evening and the day is now far spent.' So he went in to stay with them.* ***When he was at table with them, he took the bread and blessed and broke it and gave it to them.*** *And their eyes were opened, and they recognized him. And he vanished from their sight*" *(Luke 24:28-31 ESV)*. When we see Jesus in our circumstance it makes sense; we find peace, and we want more. No matter what I am going through, when the presence shows up, I am grateful, and it makes me appreciate whatever brought His presence in spite of not understanding.

You may be thinking, but how does that apply to me? Remember I told you that we pray in faith and trust Him for the outcome. This is the example. Finally those seated around the table started to see it through Jesus's perspective. This is the unnatural way to see; this is looking through the eyes of faith. Jesus was on a mission the entire time He walked this earth. Everything He suffered was for you and me. No one could have prayed Him from the cross even though He was innocent of any wrong doing. In the natural, it looked like an unjust murder, but looking at the heavenly purpose it was the very access to open heaven. When we can take our circumstance and surrender our expectation, we can start to embrace His perspective. My sorrow at my dad's death instantly turned into gratitude and thankfulness for such a powerful life of influence and hope. My dad was saved. I was praying for healing. The Scriptures say I can believe for that; however, if I see it through the eyes of plan and purpose and if His death causes 4 people to be saved and 15 people's faith to be strengthened, then that is what I must see and value like God does. I can say confidently that I feel this way. This comes by asking God to transform our thinking to the big kingdom picture.

In order for us to press on and keep a heavenly perspective, we have to settle the regret of it not panning out like we wanted. We can't change the big picture, and we shouldn't want to. Only when we understand He is perfect and so are His ways can we push regret far from us. I have not experienced this in every circumstance in life, but I have packed my bags and am heading there. Grieving a situation is an adjustment to a new earthly reality, but cemented in the truth of a true heavenly perspective. I believe healing will come wrapped in this truth.

Do I miss my dad? A thousand times yes, but when I begin to miss him, I just dwell on the fact that the return of the Lord can happen at any moment, and we can be reunited. Meanwhile, I don't grieve for him. He is in perfect peace and wouldn't come back if I begged him. That gives me peace and hope. I can grieve one-sided and not grieve as though he is suffering or missing me. I believe heaven is a perfect environment. I don't believe there is sorrow there of any kind. I also know that time is not measured as it is here. One day is as a thousand years in heaven. From the heavenly vantage point, I am sure my dad won't really have time to miss us even if he could. If you dwell on the "what if's" or regrets, how can you move past any situation? That is the devil's leash. You may have a saved loved one who has passed on, and you have regret that you didn't get to say something before they passed or didn't get to make something right. Can I tell you to be free? They don't hold onto that in heaven; it would be sin. I believe the Lord wipes those negative things from their minds. It wouldn't be heaven if that person was there sad and depressed. Trust me, the glory of God will not allow negativity to chain your loved one. My friend, grab onto the goodness of God in every situation.

Let me give you another example that I learned first-hand from my experience with my dad. One day close to the end, I saw my dad weeping, and as I saw him adjusting himself in his chair, he was saying over and over, "I can't believe how good God is to me. I can't believe it. I can't believe it." He felt God's goodness through all the people who were coming to visit him and telling him how much they were inspired by his perseverance. How can someone say that when cancer is eating up his physical body? I can tell you how- by the power of God. He saw the risen Lord in his circumstance, in his boat, and that is what counts when we face life-threatening situations. He was overwhelmed by the help my mother and he were receiving.

God brings comfort through people. My expectation is physical healing, but God's perspective may be the solidity of my family and the faith of my dad's closest friend. Friend, our faith is the only thing that will last. My dad's body may have physically decayed, but his spirit was soaring in the grace of God here and through the clouds into the third heaven. We can do the same through anything we may experience. Through the death of our expectations, hope can rise on the wings of His perfect will.

With Cleopas and these followers, the Lord allowed the veiling until they began to see His perspective. Many of us remain in a state of grief or discouragement because of an undesired outcome and God wants to resurrect an understanding for us. When they let go of the disappointment and let go of their own perspective, they saw Jesus. In the breaking came the seeing. When He broke the bread, and those around the table could see, they began to burn with desire to share Christ and what He had done with everyone around them. Look at these verses, "*They said to each other, 'Did not our hearts burn within us while he talked to us on the road, while he opened to us the Scriptures?' And they rose that same hour and returned to Jerusalem. And they found the eleven and those who were with them gathered together, saying, 'The Lord has risen indeed, and has appeared to Simon!' Then they told what had happened on the road, and how he was known to them in the breaking of the bread" (Luke 24:32-35 ESV).* In the burning came the going. Once again we see, just like with the women in the story, their revelation sent them out to those who were hurting in the same way as they were. This revelation sent these two out as well.

What about those who don't experience the Road to Emmaus revelation and they go straight back to fishing? You may be saying, but what if I lost it and got angry with the Lord? The resurrection is for you also. Friend, I did that with the miscarriages, if you remember. The Lord taught me something that I would come to apply in the death of my dad. I think if I had not gone through such massive amounts of heartbreak in that area, the death of my dad would have destroyed me. Our resurrected King is the Great Restorer when we blow it. Jesus doesn't want us to live in bondage to the guilt of our true feelings in our disappointments. He doesn't want to throw us aside when we get angry with Him in our frustration either.

The greatest example we see is with Jesus's friend Peter. I know some of you may be like Peter was; the disappointment was too much. You have been serving Jesus for a while, but you are spiritually side tracked. No one knows it, but the disappointment you have faced has been too much. It has tipped you over, and you are stuck on your side and unable to walk in the power of God. Jesus is not satisfied with you just serving Him, just coming to church. He wants all of you, those parts He had before the walls came up. Maybe you didn't walk away physically, but emotionally you are crippled in disappointment, and you are hiding. Jesus came to the Cross to die for you, and He will not leave you until He restores you out of your disappointment. Before Jesus left this earth, he ensured that His friend was restored. Look again at Peter. He was passionate, and he loved Jesus. He was always jumping the gun, so to speak; he would speak before he knew the facts. A week passed since the death of his Lord, his best friend. The pain and guilt of denying Christ was still a vivid memory. He had not handled the situation like he boasted he would. Imagine how it was replayed over and over in his mind. Peter had been with Jesus at least twice at this point.

Let's look at the scene at the sea of Galilee in John's Gospel: "*Simon Peter said to them, 'I am going fishing.' They said to him, 'We will also come with you.' They went out, and got into the boat; and that night they caught nothing. But when the day was now breaking, Jesus stood on the beach; yet the disciples did not know that it was Jesus. Jesus therefore said to them, 'Children, you do not have any fish, do you?' They answered Him, 'No.' And He said to them, 'Cast the net on the right-hand side of the boat, and you will find a catch.' They cast therefore, and then they were not able to haul it in because of the great number of fish. That disciple therefore whom Jesus loved said to Peter, 'It is the Lord.' And so when Simon Peter heard that it was the Lord, he put his outer garment on (for he was stripped for work), and threw himself into the sea" (John 21:3-7 NASB).* Peter jumped into the water not because he was afraid of condemnation, but he wanted to be restored to His Lord, Master, and best friend. Peter had been carrying this heavy guilt, and Jesus knew it. Can I pause here and say the Lord knows if you are mad at Him, and he is taking the first step in restoration? Jesus had not done anything to Peter, but Jesus initiated the breakfast, as he did nothing to you no matter what your perception is. Nevertheless, His arms are open saying, "Come and talk with me, and let me restore us as we were." A fresh encounter with the Lord will always bring a new beginning. I want to show you something in the Greek translation of this restoration. I have inserted the Greek words for love in the text to help you understand what was being said and why. Let's look again at the account in the book of John: *"When they had finished breakfast, Jesus said to Simon Peter, 'Simon, son of John, do you love* **(agape)** *me more than these?' He said to him, 'Yes, Lord; you know that I love* **(phileo)** *you.' He said to him, "Feed my lambs." He said to him a second time, 'Simon, son of John, do you love* **(agape)** *me?' He said to him, 'Yes, Lord; you know that I love* **(phileo)** *you.' He said to him, 'Tend my sheep.' He said to him the third time, 'Simon, son of John, do you love* **(phileo)** *me?' Peter was grieved because he said to him the third time, 'Do you love* **(phileo)** *me?' and he said to him, 'Lord, you know everything; you know that I love* **(phileo)** *you.' Jesus said to him, 'Feed my sheep'" (John 21:15-17 ESV).* Jesus called him Simon (the name before Jesus renamed him Peter); Jesus did this as a reminder that Peter was acting like his old self. The name Simon pierced his heart because Jesus had renamed him Peter meaning "rock" which spoke of the potential Jesus saw in him and the change in Peter's destiny. Jesus asked him three times if he loved Him because he had denied Him three times. In verse 15, Jesus says agape. In other words do you love me in an unconditional, godly, sacrificial, totally committed love? Peter says, "I phileo you." It was brotherly fondness. Why? His failure was telling him that he didn't love Jesus unconditionally and sacrificially. Guilt was still speaking. Peter was no longer boasting. In verse 16, Jesus says agape again. Peter responds with phileo again. Peter was now aware of his limitations. In verse 17, Jesus uses Peter's word phileo in the third question. Peter knew Jesus was using His omniscience because Peter tells Him, "Lord, you already know all things, I phileo you," and Jesus agreed. I think Peter was grieved because he knew he wanted to love with an agape love, and that should also be the cry of our hearts. You see, Peter's zeal kept him from seeing who he really was.

As long as there is water to walk on or a miracle to see, passion may look like unconditional love. Agape comes from laying down the internal struggle with Jesus that no one sees, and it is not until we deal with what is stifling us that we will transcend into agape. This is the whole point in the devastations, in the not understanding, in the blowing it; this is where the resurrection can be seen because God is for us. In spite of what we go through, His plan is perfect, sacred; no matter how we respond, or hold out, He is always pursuing us. My good friend Steve Himel kept drilling into my head throughout all of the miscarriages, "Kelly, I can't explain why this keeps happening, but I know God is for you." I have come to know that. God is always pursuing us no matter what we are going through. He did it by ripping the veil. He did it by walking next to us when we don't understand. He did it in our restoration when were unfaithful because of fear or disappointment. After the miscarriages, the Lord in a sense asked me the same thing. I felt I had merely showed phileo love. That's all I had. Those miscarriage disappointments were a phileo wall I put up. Jesus kept on pursuing me through every fit, every outburst, and every spiteful word I would scream into the heavens for which

I am not proud. It was preparing me for what I would learn in the loss of my dad. I can say that I went through this devastation with (agape) love for Him. I have learned sometimes all we can do is bring God all of our dreams, our molds, and say, "God, this is what I have. This is where I am." That is all the Lord requires. Similarly, He asked Adam, "Where are you?" When we fall, He shows up. In the devastation, He shows up. In the not understanding, He's explaining. In the times we lose it, He restores. How about you? Eventually Peter's life showed that he agaped the Lord because history tells us he died for Him. I say all of this because we often think we are sold out to Christ, but the Lord knows how we love Him. We just need to know for ourselves. Jesus will always address the issues in our lives to restore us, and He will address what's in our hearts at the very moment, with the goal of bringing us to agape love, which is how He loves us.

As I close out this chapter and book, His resurrection means our resurrection. Paul wrote, "*So you see, just as death came into the world through a man, now the resurrection from the dead has begun through another man. Just as everyone dies because we all belong to Adam, everyone who belongs to Christ will be given new life. But there is an order to this resurrection: Christ was raised as the first of the harvest; then all who belong to Christ will be raised when he comes back" (1 Cor 15:21-23 NLT).* Also the book of Acts says, "*And when he had said these things, as they were looking on, he was lifted up, and a cloud took him out of their sight. And while they were gazing into heaven as he went, behold, two men stood by them in white robes, and said, 'Men of Galilee, why do you stand looking into heaven? This Jesus, who was taken up from you into heaven, will come in the same way as you saw him go into heaven'"* *(Acts 1:9-11 ESV).* No matter what we face here, His resurrection means we will enter into perfect peace. If you lost love ones here, you will follow their physical bodies into heaven.

I will close with my favorite verses in all of Scripture; in Paul's letter to the Thessalonians, he wrote, "*For if we believe that Jesus died and rose again, even so God will bring with Him those who sleep in Jesus. For this we say to you by the word of the Lord, that we who are alive and remain until the coming of the Lord will by no means precede those who are asleep. For the Lord Himself will descend from heaven with a shout, with the voice of an archangel, and with the trumpet of God. And the dead in Christ will rise first. Then we who are alive and remain shall be caught up together with them in the clouds to meet the Lord in the air. And thus we shall always be with the Lord. Therefore comfort one another with these words" (1 Thessalonians 4:14-18 NKJV).* Listen to me friend, ride it out. No matter what is crippling you right now, it will pale in comparison to that day that is on the horizon. Resurrection morning is coming.

I want to close out this book with a prayer. You may not know Jesus as your personal Savior today. I want to give you an opportunity to receive him right now. Repeat this prayer after me. The prayer will not save you. It is the belief in your heart as you say these words that saves you.

Dear heavenly Father, I come to You in the name of Your son Jesus. I confess that I have sinned and broken Your laws.

I repent and ask You to forgive me. I put my faith in what Jesus did at the cross. I acknowledge that He died the death I should have died. I believe in my heart that Jesus is Your son. I confess with my mouth that Jesus is my Lord, and I believe in my heart that You raised Him from the dead. Please help me live for You all the days of my life. Thank You for saving me. I am a child of the Most High God. Amen!

Printed in the United States
By Bookmasters